WEST ROW GIRL
A pre-war Suffolk Childhood

by
Una Ellen Jenkins - neé Norman - 2007

Best Wishes

Una

Cover Photograph Supplied by Dave Kindred

First Published in 2007

ISBN 978-0-9557543-0-2

Printed in Great Britain by
The Lavenham Press Ltd,
Water Street, Lavenham, Suffolk

For my brother Don

ACKNOWLEDGEMENTS

I owe a special debt of gratitude to my brother Don for his help and support and to the generosity of Natalie Wheatley, who gave so freely of her time and advice. I am particularly grateful to my son Tim who with his love of history helped and encouraged me so much. He spent many hours scanning and arranging the photographs, which were so freely given by relations and friends. My thanks also to the Bury Free Press for giving permission to use the photographs of the Royal Visit to Mildenhall Aerodrome.

My thanks also to Mike Delph, our computer wizard, who was always on hand if I was in trouble.

My heartfelt thanks to my husband Don for without his help and enthusiasm this book would have not been finished.

Finally to my granddaughter Mimi, whose idea it was in the first place, 'because she knew nothing of my childhood'.

I have written this book from my memories, which are transient things, so if there are any errors or omissions my sincere apologies.

WEST ROW GIRL

A Personal Narrative of life in a Village in Suffolk

In the 1930's

©Una Ellen Jenkins – neé Norman - 2007

My Mother holding me in 1928

INTRODUCTION

This is a story of a year in the life of a small girl living in West Row, a village on the edge of the fens in Suffolk. These were the days when children were safe on their own and people left their doors open and nothing was stolen.

My father, Herbert Norman

My father was one of 6 boys born to my grandparents, James and Anne Norman. My grandfather was a horse dealer and at one time kept a public house called the Pear Tree, in the village. The 6 brothers were very close, all living in the village and meeting often. I can never remember any bad feeling between them. My father was a general agricultural labourer. He worked on the fen drainage dykes in the winter, harvesting in the summer, on the traction engines (or steaming as it was known) in the autumn - in fact every job that was required on the land in that early mechanical age. He also had a large allotment rented from the Council where he spent many happy hours planting and tending all the vegetables his growing family needed. He also kept pigs and chickens so the whole family was well provided for by this highly industrious man.

My Mother Rachel

My mother bore 10 children and for the latter part of her life was unwell. My memory of her is of an intelligent, kindly and friendly person who had, however, much to bear in a life that saw her two brothers, Arthur and James, killed in the Great War, whilst serving in the 6th Suffolk Regiment. She also lost twins at birth, together with my sister Agnes and my brother Kenneth, who both died in childhood - such were the hardships of the time. The surviving children were Victor, the eldest, Elsie, Alec, Leslie, Don and the youngest - Una, the author, who was born in 1928.

**My Parents on their Wedding Day, with Aunt Nellie and Uncle James
(Who was killed in the Great War).**

My Parents on their Wedding Day

Friday Street, West Row, showing the Fish Shop at the far end of the Street

West Row is a village situated close to the small market town of Mildenhall, on the edge of the fens in Suffolk. In 1931 it had a population of approximately 1600 people.[1] Residents at this time were mostly farmers and agricultural workers, with their families. The village had numerous shops; a bakery, two butchers, a fish and chip shop, several pubs, a village hall and a well-attended school. The headmaster of the school, Mr. Mothersole, was highly regarded by the whole village. Parents, many of whom could not read or write, looked to him to teach their children the three R's. The village had its own policeman of course, for there were a few cars getting about and strangers were beginning to appear.

---

[1] In the 1931 Census, West Row Parish was united with Mildenhall. It was not separated until 1971

The Baptist Chapel

Religion played a large part in village life and there were three chapels and a church. My family were Baptists and Reverend Fendick, the Pastor, lived in the manse across the road from the chapel.

Rev & Mrs Fendick

The Baptists were probably the largest religious community in West Row, although there were the Wesleyans and a strict Baptist group who worshipped in the barn chapel. There was also the small C of E church St Peters, which was situated close to the village green – so with each denomination having its own pastor, or vicar, we were well catered for spiritually. There were also lay preachers and deacons of course and I well remember the Bacon family who were both (and who I will write about later).

West Row War Memorial and St Peter's Church

There were 35 young men from the village killed in the Great War and their memorial stands on The Green in front of St Peter's church, it seems such a waste of young lives. I was born long after this and it was only when I was engaged in research, prior to writing this narrative that I discovered each man returning from serving in the armed services during the Great War, was given the opportunity to rent a small holding, of approximately 20 acres, from the council. Many took advantage of this scheme and worked the land for the rest of their lives, becoming prosperous farmers in their own right.

After the war the village returned to its peaceful pursuits. Although it became increasingly more difficult for labourers to exist on agricultural wages alone, because of the industrious tending of allotments and gardens, the extreme deprivation suffered in the larger towns, was not experienced here. There was also an excellent community spirit and help was always at hand for the needy. This is the time when I was born and this is the story of my life in the village of West Row and of the wonderful, generous people who helped and succoured me.

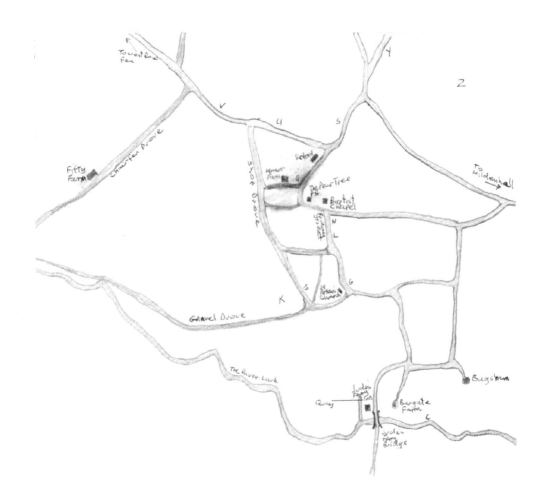

C = Bargate, where we swam   G = Our House   J = Shop Drove

K = The Allotments   L = Hinds' Shop   N = The Manse

S = The Well Pond   U = Thistley Green.

V = My sister Elsie's first cottage after she was married.

Y = Footpath to Airfield   Z = The Airfield

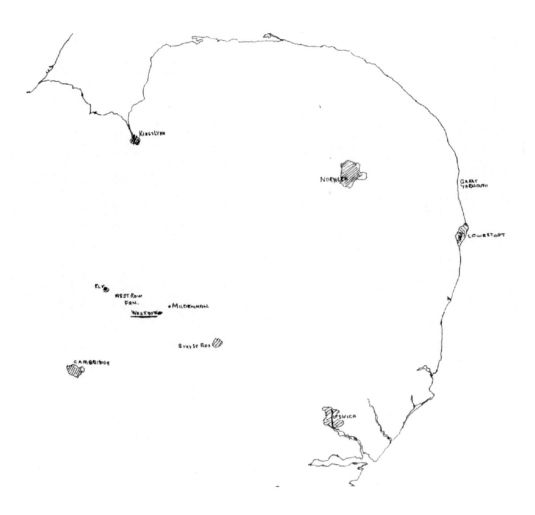

KingsLynn

Norwich

Great
Yarmouth

Lowestoft

Ely
WestRow
Fen.
WestRow   Mildenhall

Bury St Eds

Cambridge

Ipswich

CHAPTER 1

CHRISTMAS

Christmas day in our family began with a combined opening of presents, (which took some time because there were so many of us) but being the youngest I was always first. On Christmas Eve I had hung my stocking on the end of the bed and I was very excited in the morning to find it full of goodies and lovely things to eat – including a large orange in the toe.

I remember one year my sister Elsie ran upstairs to me, to tell me that there was a large parcel in the living room. She did not know what it could be – but it was from Father Christmas. I ran down stairs with Elsie and, sure enough, there was a big parcel with a label with my name on. I tore off the pretty paper the parcel was wrapped in and there to my surprise and joy was a little blue Fairy Cycle – I just could not believe it. I thought that it was the best bicycle in the whole world – it had a leather saddle, a wicker basket on the handlebars, together with a bell, a blue pump and a little leather bag full of tools, hanging behind the saddle.

To say that I was overjoyed was to put it mildly and I was really impatient to ride my new bicycle as soon as the chores were finished - needless to say, I had many falls, cuts and bruises before I managed to ride it. I really loved that little blue bicycle and rode it everywhere in the village and it lasted me for years. I wonder what happened to it. On reflection, I also now wonder who actually bought the bicycle for me. Of course, at the time I thought it had come from Father Christmas and nobody in the family has ever let on but I suspect, that it was my brother Vic. I am sure that my dad would not have bought me a bicycle without buying one for Leslie and Don.

Vic by now was attending the local Livestock Market at Bury St Edmunds and he always brought me a little present on his return. When he came home he had his hand in his coat pocket and would slowly bring it out and give me a little present – sometimes chocolate, sweets and sometimes a novelty. When he came in, my attention would focus on his pocket and he never disappointed me. At Easter Vic always bought me a huge chocolate Easter egg, with coloured icing flowers on the front. I was reluctant to break this lovely egg but, when I did, I shared it out with my brothers and saved a special piece, with the icing flowers, for Vic.

Christmas breakfast in our house consisted of a joint of salt pork and one of salt beef cooked, I believe, in our copper on Christmas Eve. I remember it was delicious and my brothers ate what seemed to me to be a tremendous amount, when they returned from feeding the stock – they were no doubt very hungry on such a cold winter morning (as the temperature at Christmas always seemed to be in those days).

Christmas was a very happy time for everyone, especially the children, for we all enjoyed singing the old carols when we went to the service in the Sunday School on Christmas morning. There was of course the added attraction of an orange and apple after the service was over. Quite where these gifts came from I am not sure, but all the children received them and they were greatly looked forward to. It really doesn't seem very much of a gift in these more affluent days but in the 1930's it seemed like manna from heaven.

We walked to Sunday School for there were few cars in the village. The roads were really very muddy from all the farm machinery and the horses that used them. All the children had to wear sturdy shoes and carefully wipe them before they went into the chapel. When we returned home after Sunday School it was time to think of the Christmas Dinner. This was very different from today as turkeys were a 'thing of the future' and most people had large joints of mutton. The lambs born in the spring were not slaughtered as they are today. They were kept and fattened, over the summer and autumn, ready to be eaten at Christmas. There was a goodly supply of vegetables too from dad's allotment and also a large Christmas pudding that had been maturing for five or six weeks.

My mother made several large Christmas Puddings in late November and they were a great favourite with us all. At the mixing stage, each of us would have a stir and a wish (which had to be kept secret or the wish would not be granted) and two or three silver thru'peny pieces were then dropped into the mixture. Basins were then filled and the tops covered with greaseproof paper and a linen cover. There was much speculation about who would be the lucky recipient of the silver and we all chewed our spoonfuls of pudding meticulously, to make sure that we did not, inadvertently, swallow the prize. Aunt Annie always cheated a little bit at this stage because, when visitors or special guests came, she would push a silver thru'peny piece into their portion to ensure they were the lucky ones.

With so many large puddings (and they were large), my mother found the best way to cook them was to use the copper, in which she washed the clothes. The puddings had to be steamed for eight hours and the copper was the only utensil large enough to cook them properly. I know today this does not seem to be too hygienic but we all ate the puddings and did not come to any harm.

After steaming for eight hours, the puddings were stored in the pantry and allowed to mature for at least a month. On Christmas Day, the chosen pudding was then steamed again to heat it thoroughly and when it was turned out of the basin it looked wonderful – being a beautiful dark brown colour and having an unforgettable aroma. I still make my puddings to this recipe.[2] Please do use my recipe if you wish – you will not be disappointed. Today you will not need to use the copper though – a humble saucepan and steamer will suffice. Remember, however, that it is essential to steam the puddings for eight hours - and, do not forget to wish when you are mixing the ingredients.

We stored the apples picked in the autumn in the garden shed, where they were laid out on a shelf and covered with a sack to protect them from the frost. I can remember running across to the shed on many a bitter winters' evening for an apple, then hurrying back to sit in front of the fire to carry on reading my latest book. I was an avid reader from an early age. One of my presents at Christmas was always a book, sometimes two or three and my sister often said to me "that it is a pity you can't find something better to do, for you always have your head stuck in a book." I did find something to do too, because I learned to knit and embroider and this stood me in good stead in the years to come. I still have a pyjama case from those early days which I embroidered painstakingly with the word PYJAMAS in red and pink and green and surrounded by green and pink flowers.

Anyway, to return to Christmas Day - after dinner and when the women of the house did the mound of washing up, those of us who were not completely worn out from the huge dinner would go walking. Although I seem to remember that the boys would rarely join in for they had their own pursuits.

My dad was not a drinker but his one indulgence was at Christmas time. He would buy a bottle of whisky and a bottle of port wine. The whisky he would drink in his tea, as was the custom, and I remember the boys also being given their tea with a teaspoon of whisky 'to enliven it' – I too was offered this beverage but I did not like that nasty stuff in my tea. On Christmas night dad would pour himself a glass of the port and would sit and chat with us around the table. One year, to my surprise, he poured out a small glass

---

[2] See Appendix 2 for the recipe.

for my mother, who we had never seen drink alcohol before. I remember her sitting at the table sipping the wine and eating a plain biscuit. It was lovely seeing her enjoying Christmas and a glass of port was to become a regular treat for her.

Soon after Christmas, in the New Year, a party was arranged by the Chapel members for all the children who attended the Sunday School. This was a really big party with a huge Christmas tree reaching to the ceiling and decorated beautifully, with a present for all the children tied on the tree. Tea was served upstairs in the 'Bird Cage'[3] (where the Anniversary was held in the spring), on large trestle tables covered with white cloths. The tables were loaded with sandwiches and fancy cakes and cups of tea were served from large urns and brought to us by the many helpers who had been enlisted.

Sitting with us at the party was Mr. Sturgeon, who was a favourite of the children. He was a great teller of fascinating tales, which kept us all spellbound. They were of course stories of family life and of adventures with a moral undertone - for Mr. Sturgeon was a lay preacher of some repute in the community. He was very prone to be the subject of practical jokes - an example being when he was so busy telling his stories, that he pretended not to notice that his cake was spirited away by a small hand. He was obliged to take another when it was offered. This happened time and again and we laughed and laughed. Looking back, in hindsight, I realise that he was playing games with us but at the time we were beside ourselves waiting for his cake to vanish and for the next one to be taken.

After tea we were all gathered together for games – 'Blind Man's Bluff,' 'Pin the Tail on the Donkey,' 'Musical Chairs,' 'Postman's Knock,' 'Oranges and Lemons' and many more. Simple games perhaps but they taught us how to mix together and to make new friends. When we were red faced with excitement and just about exhausted, there would be a mighty knocking on the door. We would all fall silent because we had a good idea of who was waiting outside.

One of the ladies opened the door and in strode Father Christmas, ringing his bell, magnificent in his red robes and flowing white beard. He had presents for everyone in his sack and no one was left out. How did he know who was there, we wondered? But he did know, and we were all called to go and shake his hand and receive our present. The wonder of it all is with me still. Trudging home in the dark clutching our gifts is a lasting memory for me and of the wonderful spirit of Christmas conjured up by those good-hearted folk who loved children.

---

[3] The 'Bird Cage' was a gallery overlooking the Chapel where children performed on the Anniversary.

CHAPTER 2

THE NEW YEAR

Strangely enough, the passing of the old year was not celebrated in the village, as far as I can remember, but quite what the grown ups were about I was not always aware. There were lots of parties, when people visited each other but in our family the gathering round the wireless to listen to the chimes of Big Ben would not arrive for some years.

The Well Pond

New Year came and went and we were soon plunged into the harshness of winter. Nowadays, it seems impossible to believe, that the Fens would freeze solidly for weeks on end and that nearly all the able bodied males kept ice skates, ready to take part in the annual racing on the frozen waterways. Winners were great heroes who were lauded throughout the area. I suspect that many wagers were won and lost and much money changed hands. Even today, people still remember the names of the top skaters, now long gone of course - they were the local heroes of their day. For the less venturesome we also had the well pond in the village, where the children skated, if they had skates – or, if not, merely ran and slid across the ice.

Winters then, were much more severe than now and everyone had the dual problems of keeping warm at home and when out and about. The children all had winter clothes, woollen vests, warm jerseys, hats, gloves, scarves and some, an oddly named liberty bodice, a soft and fleecy garment without sleeves. They were worn over the vest and buttoned down the front - both little boys and girls wore them and they certainly helped us to keep warm.

Of course, there was no electricity or gas in the village and for water; we relied upon the well in the garden. At home, the downstairs rooms were heated by a Combination Range, which served as both cooker and heater. It was made of iron and worked efficiently, but was very prone to rust if neglected. A daily chore was the black-leading of the stove, which was carried out by the housewives, who took great pride in having their stove shining and bright.

The fire grate was on the right hand side of the range. We could place saucepans on a cast iron ring, when the fire was lit and burning well. The ring could also be removed if one wanted to boil a kettle quickly and a special tool was provided for this.

The Range, as I mentioned before, also provided warmth in the living room and many a long winters' evening was spent by our family toasting our toes and telling simple stories of happenings in the village.

The oven was on the lower left hand side of the Range and an ingeniously linked lever (which diverted the flames from the fire and deflected them over the oven and then up the chimney), controlled the heat. If this sounds a bit hit and miss to the modern cook, perhaps it was but the results were usually good because the art of tending a fire was a skill learned, by all budding housewives, at their mothers' knee.

It seems fantastic now to think of women cooking each day for large families, totally without running water, electricity or refrigerators. However, an advantage then, was that even the smallest of cottages had a stone floored pantry and, in some cases, cellars, to help keep food fresh. In addition, many households also had a wooden or metal meat safe, with a mesh front, which was either kept outside in the shadiest corner of the yard, or in the pantry.

Our cottage was blessed with an open hearth in the kitchen, which was a great boon. It supplemented the Range in heating water in a large black iron kettle on a trivet by the fire and was also of great assistance in cooking the masses of vegetables and stews, which my mother prepared.

Houses were smaller then, and families were larger, so there were more people living in a much smaller area than the present day. This helped to keep us warm in the daytime – most bedrooms, however, were very cold in the winter - central heating was a luxury many years in the future. Nevertheless, some means had to be found for warmth and, although most cottages did have at least one fireplace upstairs, generally, the updraft was quite poor in the chimneys – particularly if the wind was strong and in the wrong direction. I think we thought it was better to be cold, than suffocated by smoke.

A simple solution to the problem of keeping warm was that we all had 'featherbeds' filled with goose feathers which were beautifully soft and warm. Stone hot water bottles were also filled from a large black iron kettle, which was kept simmering on the hob. Covering us we also had flannelette sheets, lots of woollen blankets, an eiderdown and, finally, a counterpane - usually of a white woven chequered material with tassels. We were thus snug and warm in our beds, despite the windows being covered by the patterns of frost on cold winter mornings. Getting up in the morning, though, was not a leisurely activity on a cold winter's morning!

The long winter evenings were a challenge for idle hands as, of course, there was no television. We did have our crystal set and earphones but it was only possible for, at most, two of us to listen at any one time. When my brother Don bought the first radio (or wireless as we called it then) that we could all sit around as a family, it was a revelation that changed our lives. He bought it from the shop in Mildenhall and it certainly caused a great stir in the family.

I remember the wireless well, for it was my job to carry the accumulator (which was a battery filled with acid), to Tom Pamment's cycle repair shed in the village to be charged. We had two accumulators - I collected the fully charged one and brought it home for dad to change over for the semi discharged one, which I then took back to be recharged for next week. I remember those accumulators very well for they were heavy, with china handles on the metal carrying case, and 'Exide' stamped on the glass container. Woe betide me if I spilt any of the acid on my clothes, for it quickly burnt a hole in anything it touched. I wonder if young children would be sent on such hazardous errands today.

Tom Pamment was inclined to be a grumpy old man who, I think, delighted in intimidating everyone, including little girls. He walked with a limp and wore greasy dark overalls; a cap and he always had dirty, oily hands. It was said in the village, that he only shaved on Sundays for Chapel but I found that he had a heart of gold and I liked him and I think he liked me too. I would chatter away to him and he would growl back but with a twinkle in his eye. Charging an accumulator was six pence and, with the average wage of thirty shillings a week, he must soon have been a wealthy man for there were many wireless sets in the village in no time.

Tom Pamment's shed was like an Aladdin's cave full of wireless parts, with wires and big clips and lights and fuses and huge bottles of acid and distilled water, packed in straw. It was all very scary for a little girl and I think I chattered away to him to calm my nerves. He also repaired bicycles and the shed was packed with wheels, frames, tyres and all manner of things required in a cycle repair shop.

We had the wireless but our winter chores still had to be done and one of these was the making of our pegged rugs. Many women were highly skilled in designing and making them and the children helped by cutting up strips of material from old clothes and any other material to hand. These strips were then pushed into a sacking base with a special tool called a peg and then knotted in place to form a rug of any size. Our mothers originated many designs using the various colours from all the materials we found. It was great fun, especially when the latest rug was finished and we tried to see where our old jersey or vest appeared. These rugs were used all around the house but with a special one for the living room fireplace.

So the long winter evenings passed with our embroidery, knitting and reading but spring was soon upon us. A sure sign that it was not far away was when we could have tea in daylight on the second Sunday in February. Meal times were strictly adhered to as families always sat down to eat together - I suppose it was a tradition fostered by the need to feed stock at regular times. I think that it was also very necessary for families to gather together and talk, not always amicably I may add, but I witnessed many a problem, real or imagined, sorted out over the dining table.

In the evenings, the whole family often gathered around the fireside and chatted for hours about the people from the village and how each family and individual was related. These long discussions were probably an echo from times when nobody in the village could read or write. They were a form of oral history by which people could pass on knowledge to the younger generation and underline roles and relationships. When I was staying with aunt Annie, the same thing happened and I suspect that this was a common practice in all families at that time. There are a few occasions today when families enjoy these discussions but will they continue in our more fragmented society?

CHAPTER 3

THE LIVESTOCK

My father was an industrious man with a large family to feed and, as with other heads of household in the village, he was obliged to keep a selection of animals, to supply essential supplements to our diet and income. In today's world, a trip to the supermarket would suffice but, in the mid thirties, when wages for agricultural labourers were a mere 30 shillings per week, it was necessary to maximise all sources of income and food production. We kept chickens, pigs, rabbits and goats; chickens were used both for their eggs and meat; rabbits and pigs were for the table and goats for their milk – which, even in those days, was considered to be of great benefit to children.

Una (in pram) with an early picture of brothers Leslie and Don

My dad was very worried about giving the young children in his family unpasteurised milk because of the dangers of tuberculosis – a widespread disease that was, at the time, known as consumption. He kept the goats until we were considered to be mature enough to drink cows milk. Milk from the local farmer was available, which was collected from the farm in a jug each day. When a cow calved, the first milk from the animal was called 'beeslams.' This milk was rich in protein and made the most marvellous custards and puddings and was given to the older children, when available.

All this stock required hard work to be kept healthy and well fed. The pigs were kept in styes in the garden and the chickens in a large moveable hen house and run. The rabbits were kept in hutches on a stretch of grass close by. The goats were milked and fed in the morning, then were walked to Shop Drove, some way from the house. The goats were then tethered with a leather collar and chain to spikes driven into the ground. They spent most of their waking hours in the drove, being walked back to our garden in the evening, where they were fed, milked again and then put in their shed for the night.

A later picture of brothers Don and Leslie

My brothers helped my father before they left for either work or school. All the food had to be prepared each day and the sheds and styes cleaned and the animals given fresh straw and water. The rabbits had to be fed and their hutches kept clean; eggs had to be collected and cleaned before the hens were fed and, of course, all the stock had to be fed, watered and bedded down, every evening. This was a year round task and all the family shared in the looking after the stock. My job was looking after the chickens and, the part I most liked, was when the eggs hatched in the spring. I couldn't wait to see the little yellow chicks running around.

Mr. Vic Bassett, from Mildenhall – who worked for Woollard's, a small egg wholesaler, collected any surplus eggs. We also had two butchers in the village – Mr. Frost, who was a pork butcher and Jessie Clark, a general butcher. Animals for our own use would be slaughtered at home but, if the butcher purchased the animals, he would collect them and they were slaughtered at the butchery.

When we had too many chickens or rabbits, we sent the surplus to be sold at the market in Bury St Edmunds and one year, I remember, that dad bred some rabbits especially to be shown at the Christmas Livestock Market. My brother Vic bought them from my father before they were sent to market, to add to the ones he was sending himself - he had just started breeding his own animals – encouraged by my father who thought that Vic seemed to have a flair for market trading. Of course he bought them at a favourable price from dad, who avoided the trouble of getting them to market. Imagine his feelings when one of his rabbits won first prize and Vic was awarded 5 shillings - which he steadfastly refused to hand over.

My Dad at Bury Market in later years

My brother Vic, with two friends, on his motorbike and sidecar

My brother Vic in later years

My brother Vic went on to become a very successful market gardener and, at one time, owned two farms and a large quantity of property and land. Mr. Mothersole the headmaster of the village school had foretold that Vic would be a successful businessman and that one day, Vic would show him around his own farm.   Some years later, the headmaster's prediction came true when Vic took him around his farm in Essex.

CHAPTER 4

CHILDHOOD

The Road Sweeper: Charlie Hurst

In the nineteen thirties there were few cars in the village and most people either travelled by train, omnibus, bicycle, or on foot. There were of course numerous horses and carts - used for both fieldwork and for the odd trip to Mildenhall Market. There were also many ponies and traps which were a more luxurious and comfortable mode of travel. I loved to ride in my uncle Albert's pony and trap, which he kept in fine condition for many years.

With all the horses in the area there were several cleaners employed by the council to keep all the village roads clean but, as cars became more common, the job of road sweeper became redundant and most either moved to other work or retired. However, when I was young, there were a few left and we had several in West Row and one of these was a special friend of mine – his name was Charlie Hurst.

Charlie was the road sweeper for several of the village roads and he was a lovely man. Before I started school, I used to wait at our gate for him to come along our road and then I would join him on his walk through the village. I remember explaining to everyone we met that he was my friend and that I was helping him with his work. I used to chatter away to him constantly as we walked along and probably made a complete nuisance of myself. However, many years later, when I met up with him, I asked how he had put up with my constant talking. He was kind enough to say that he looked forward to reaching our house and that he was quite disappointed if I was not able to be there. How lucky I was to have known him.

Starting School

Council School, West Row.

West Row School

Exploring the village was fun and I particularly enjoyed walking all the way to school in the afternoon, to meet my brother Don. It was a good half-mile or so and, with my passion for never being late, I was often early and had to wait at the gate. It was not long before my presence was noticed and a teacher came out to find out why I was there every day. Hearing that I was waiting for my brother Don, I was, to my delight, invited inside. I was allowed to sit next to Don until the end-of-the-day bell rang – just what the other pupils thought about my presence, I never found out but I suppose my brother must have been teased when his baby sister came into the classroom to sit with him. I went to school every day after this but I cannot say that I learned an awful lot – except, perhaps, to be silent, which no doubt helped me when I started school a year or so later.

Commencing school for me was a great experience. I was five years of age and, after the adventures outlined above, was fully prepared for the hurly burly of school life. I walked to school each morning with Peggy Bacon, who lived next door, and we quickly became close friends. We were very much into Chapel life at this time and on Wednesdays we always called into the Chapel on our way home from school, for the Women's Meeting. This was held in the Sunday School and was often finished by the time we arrived but, by a strange chance, we were always in time for the generous tea the ladies of the chapel always provided for themselves.

Peggy's family were all lay preachers and she was the eldest daughter of Adolphus, whose father, Henry was the Deacon of the Chapel and a great character. On Sunday mornings and Sunday evenings, Henry would speak from the front pew, mentioning the business of the week and the happenings in the village. I can hear his sepulchral tones even now, as he read the list of births, marriages, deaths, meetings for the coming week and collections received from the previous Sunday – his intonation of POUNDS, SHILLINGS and PENCE made the congregation hang on to his every word and, no doubt, helped to persuade the more affluent, to increase the collection for the current week. He also led prayers for the sick and needy – he was, truly a good man.

Sadly, my friend Peggy's father, Adolphus (Dolph), died of cancer at an early age but his brother, Hugh, carried on the tradition of lay preaching, started by his father and elder brother – they were, all three, towers of strength for the whole community.

Henry Bacon with his son Dolph

Miss Turner, one of the teachers at West Row School, had a wonderful way with children and was very popular both with parents and her students. She was certainly my favourite teacher and this was really confirmed, when she introduced us to a book, written by Joyce Lancaster Brisley, called 'Milly Molly Mandy'[4]. She read excerpts aloud to our class every Friday and this was certainly the best lesson of the week for me.

I had to wait until the following Christmas for my own copy of this lovely book but it was top of my list of presents that I posted up the chimney to Father Christmas. On Christmas morning I was overjoyed to find the book with my Christmas stocking and I then knew that Father Christmas had definitely read my list. 'Milly Molly Mandy' remained my favourite children's book throughout my childhood - and it still is.

Everyone suffers disappointments when your plans go badly wrong and I suffered my first major disaster when still at school. It all started when Miss Turner asked me if my brother Vic would let her have a bunch of pyrethrums for her house in Mildenhall. I said that I was sure he would but I would ask him during the dinnertime break.

---

[4] 'Milly Molly Mandy' was first published in book form in 1928. The book is still in print and I have recently bought a copy for my great granddaughter – I hope she grows to love it, as I did.

After dinner I cycled to the allotments on my little blue bike and asked Vic, who was generous to a fault, and who, of course, said yes. He cut a huge bunch for me to take to her, which I tried to put in the basket on my handlebars. I quickly found that the stalks were too long, so Vic tied them to my handlebars, because I was totally unable to ride single-handed.

Off I went down the rough drove, wobbling quite a lot, as there were large potholes to avoid, but as pleased as punch to have all these flowers to give to my teacher. There is an old saying 'pride comes before a fall' and certainly it was true on that day for me. As I rode over the ruts on the drove, the flowers fell into my front wheel and in a trice they were all shredded to pieces by the spokes.

I was completely horrified by this disaster. It was too late to go back to my brother Vic and ask him for some more flowers, as I would have been late for afternoon school.   My whole world seemed to collapse and I set off for school once more, crying as I cycled along. I met a friend of my father, who stopped me and asked me what was wrong and, when I sobbingly told him, he cut off the ruined flowers and threw them in the ditch.

He tried to comfort me by saying that he was sure my teacher would understand, when I did get back to school, it seemed that she did understand because when there were no flowers on her desk, she said that she had thought afterwards that Vic probably only grew flowers to sell at the market. So I didn't tell her of my disaster and never did ......but you know, I think she knew about it all the time. It has remained my secret all my life, until now.

The Fen Children

Besides the school in West Row there was another school on Engine Drove, some way down West Row Fen. We had little to do with the pupils for the school was a long way from the village and very isolated. However, sudden changes often come to pass and, in this case, the sudden change was that the lady teacher at the Fen School decided to marry and thus she had to leave teaching. No replacement could be found to teach in this isolated school and it was decided to transfer the pupils to West Row School.

The problem was how to collect some twenty children at the same time, take them to school in the mornings, and return them home in the late afternoons. This was quite a problem for the fen roads were not exactly smooth - they were often muddy and subject to subsidence (as a result of fen drainage and the consequent shrinkage of the peat).

Mr. Jack Ingle solved the problem for he owned a four-wheeled wagon with a removable canvas top.   Two strong horses drew it, one black and one white and he could use this to collect the children, if he added long forms or benches for all the children to sit on. Somehow and somewhere a deal was struck and all 20 of the children from the Fen School descended on the West Row School. It took them the best part of an hour to make the journey to the village and another hour to get home again in the afternoon - it was a tiring day for them. Mr. Ingle's wagon was soon nicknamed the 'Stage Coach' and became a common sight in the village.

I think we thought the children from the Fen School would be a little slow on the uptake for they lived in such an isolated community but we soon found that quite the reverse was true - they were as bright as crickets and more than kept up with the best of us. We soon made friends with them and they fitted into West Row School very well.

May Dolls

The first of May was an auspicious date for the girls in the village because this was the day on which we took our dolls and teddy bears around the village, to show them off to anyone who would pay to see them.

We started early in the morning with a wicker clothes basket, which we lined with the prettiest cloth we could find. We then placed our dolls and teddy bears, in the basket, dressed in their Sunday best, and garlanded them with daisy chains and as many spring flowers we could find – mostly from the hedgerows but, occasionally, from our neighbours' gardens (if they were not looking). In the middle of the display we placed a small pot that, hopefully, would receive the money we collected, and then we covered the basket with a white tablecloth. We had a quick breakfast and then set off on our mission.

My friend and I would carry the basket around the houses in the village, knocking on doors and asking the unsuspecting householders, if they would like to see the May Dolls for which we would make a small charge. Most people would say yes and we would then lift the cloth and money would tinkle into our pot and off we would go to the next house. We were not collecting for charity, I must add, for it was understood that on this day the money was for us.

We worked hard and great was the fun and suspense when, at the end of our day, we counted our takings. We split the proceeds and, took the pennies, halfpennies and farthings down to Mrs. Clarke's shop, opposite the school, to convert into sherbet dips, gob stoppers, golden charms, lollipops, liquorice pipes and as many other exotic goodies as our takings would allow. The shop was an absolute delight with its smells of pipe tobacco, aniseed balls, cough mixture, humbugs and the image of this shop with it's wonderful variety of smells are an enduring memory. The May dolls taught us simple facts of life that one can only sell good work when it is well presented and, that it is no bad thing to be first in the market.

Empire Day

The whole school celebrated Empire Day early in May and both the staff and the pupils wore Pompom daisies in their buttonholes. Quite why we wore Bellis Pomponettes, I really can't say, but everyone in the school was expected to comply – needless to say we all did so. Dad always grew these daisies in our front garden and they were in flower at this time of the year. We always had a steady flow of children coming to call before school started. The flowers rapidly vanished into the buttonholes of the children and we all set off for school suitably attired.

The lessons that day were concentrated on the countries of the British Empire – their customs, dress, food, capitals, position on the globe etc. By the time school was finished for the day we were all very much better informed about the peoples of the Empire and filled with a patriotic fervour instilled by our teachers. We were all proud to be British and wore our Bellis Pomponettes with pride.

The Anniversary

Village life was great fun for me and one of my really lovely days was the Sunday School Anniversary. The Sunday School was built as an annex to the Baptist Chapel, in 1911, from the contributions of members of the Chapel. I believe that everyone was asked to buy at least one

brick and, as an added inducement, the bricks were inscribed with the donors' names – quite an innovation, at the time, I think. The scheme certainly worked because, after a remarkably short period of time, the required monies were raised and the Sunday School was built. The Anniversary was a concert organised by the members of the Sunday School to celebrate the opening of the school, which always took place on the second Sunday in May.

About six weeks before the day, all the children commenced rehearsals – learning the words and music of new hymns, with Mrs. Hinds, the organist and Miss Gladys Fendick, the pastor's daughter. Quite how musical we were I am not sure but a grand noise ensued and it was all great fun. Songs were performed by the most able of us and some read epics or recited poems. One performance which always sticks in my memory was the yearly contribution from my cousin Nellie – it was a long poem full of moral virtues, with orphans, hardships, misfortunes, and death – which reduced us all to tears before the end. This was a real 'tour de force' from Nellie, who remembered the lines perfectly every year – she never needed a prompt.

Cousin Nellie (rear left) with cousin Ivy (rear right)

The Sunday School Treat

Leading the Procession

The Band

As you can see, the Chapel had a great influence on all the children of the village and, one of the events that gave us the greatest pleasure and joy, was the Sunday School Treat. This occurred in early summer when, as the time of the Treat neared, there was great excitement in the congregation. There was also much coming and going, with the ladies bringing home made cakes and sausage rolls and the delivery of huge quantities of 'hot crossed buns' by the West Row Bakery. (Why hot crossed buns in early summer, I do not know but it was a tradition and they were delicious).

West Row Band

The Treat involved the children in the Sunday School being taken in wagons around all the villages in the area.   It was, I suppose, an early form of advertising for the Baptists – showing all the local villages that the children in West Row were very well looked after both physically and spiritually. The Treat entailed the villagers decorating around six large wagons with a profusion of flowers and bunting. Benches were placed in the carts and decorated boughs were fastened above the sitting area. There was also a special wagon to carry the organ and the members of the village band because all those present would be expected to sing rousing hymns on our journey through the local villages.

The horses to pull the wagons were all lent by their owners in the village and each animal was decorated and groomed to a really high standard – with the horse brasses gleaming and the harnesses dressed and cleaned. The children were all in their 'Sunday best,' as were the many parents who accompanied us.

Waiting to join the Procession

We set off in the morning with the first port of call being Beck Row – a village that, in later years, was to be the home of the Mildenhall aerodrome but, at this time, was just a small hamlet some two miles from our village. The villagers turned out in strength because they had all been informed that we were on our way. We gave them several rousing hymns, whilst resting the horses in a local field, and then, after lemonade was given to the thirsty, we set off again. This time our destination was Holywell Row – a stone's throw from Beck Row, where we were clapped and cheered again, before we set off.   We headed for Mildenhall, the local market town that boasted a gas works and a railway station with connections to London. We passed the town square, amidst much cheering and waving from the inhabitants, before we headed off again, for our final destination – Barton Mills.

We drew into a large meadow, where the horses were unharnessed, and we climbed down from the wagons. We were given lemonade and hot crossed buns by the helpers and teachers. We then had great fun playing ball games and lots of chasing about activities, to run off our energies, before the long journey back to West Row – where more organised games were scheduled in the evening.

Local lads with decorated bicycles

After the horses were rested, we all set off once again for the return journey. There were lots of boys with bicycles (dressed overall) with flowers and garlands, as were their dogs – which they had brought along for the fun. There seemed to be many more boys on bicycles than had set out from West Row but no doubt we collected quite a few on the way. We were soon back in Mildenhall but, as time was pressing, we went along West Street and then straight out of the town on the long road to West Row. Little did we know, that in just a few years, all along those peaceful fields we passed, that bombers would be standing at their dispersal bays, waiting to leave for Germany.

As we neared the Chapel there was great excitement because we were eager for tea and the organised games that were to be in the late afternoon and evening. A huge spread had been laid out for us in the Sunday School, and we all enjoyed sandwiches, a great variety of cakes and cups of tea. Afterwards, we walked to Park Farm meadow, where all kinds of games were played. The one I remember most was when Dick Rolfe, the local wheelwright, ran around the field, wearing a long black coat covered in small bags of sweets. The children chased him and, if they were able to catch him, they would pull the sweets off. He was quite artful at dodging and it was no easy task for them to catch him. He was careful though, to ensure that each child received a bag of sweets, before he ran away through the gate.

It was early summer and the evenings were long. The day had been busy and exciting from the start. This was the time when the little ones had to head home for bed. The older children stayed until dusk, before they too trundled home – the end of a perfect day.

In later years the horses and wagons were replaced by six of Mr. Morley's omnibuses and we all went to the seaside in grand style. Of course, I was a little older by that time but the pleasure was just the same. We started from the village green, where the coaches collected and we boarded in great excitement, looking forward to the day. We spent most of the day on the beach, if the weather was fine, where we paddled and played to our hearts' content. At the close of the day, we would meet at one of the seafront restaurants for a great feast of shrimps and bread and butter. We sang all the way home and arrived, tired but happy, having spent another wonderful day together. Looking back, I do not think the coaches had quite the same charm as the horses and wagons – but time moves on.

Peggy Bacon, Granny Bacon and Una walking on the Promenade

CHAPTER 5

MY SISTER ELSIE

My sister Elsie was 16 years old when I was born and I grew up under her wing. She, no doubt, was somewhat dismayed to have a younger sister appear on the scene but I remember her as an attractive young woman, very smartly dressed and something of a martinet, who helped me with growing up and learning to cope with life in West Row. She was married to Fred Taylor-Balls, a local haulage contractor, and lived, when I was a small girl, in a cottage on the street called the Green, which led to the Fens. I spent some time at their home as mum was ill and Elsie taught me to cook. She was quite excellent in the kitchen and I used to watch her for hours. She excelled in cakes and sponges, and one of my favourites was a chocolate sponge with cream filling and icing on the top. She could run a fork around the top to form ridges and decorate it with walnuts in a trice. I still follow her recipe and decorate the top of my sponges in the same way.

Elsie, holding Una with Tiny and Bubbly Hinds, outside Morley's Garage in 1930

Sometimes Elsie would let me help, mostly washing up as far as I can remember, and the lessons I learnt from her have remained with me for all my life. It must have been difficult for her to have a small sister to care for but she always looked after and protected me.

Una, Elsie, Bubbly, Ada Mackender, Rosa Morley and Tiny

Before she was married, and when I was old enough, she fitted a child seat to her bicycle to enable her to take me to meet her friends. They made a great fuss of me, I remember, and Rosa Morley, Elsie's closest friend, naturally became my friend also. Rosa was a lovely girl and she took me to meet her mother and father at their home. It was called Manor Farm and was in the centre of the village. I became a regular visitor, spending many happy hours with them.

Rosa Morley

Tragically, Rosa's days were numbered, for she died at the age of eighteen, from pneumonia. This was a common illness, and without the help of penicillin and antibiotics, which were unknown at the time, treatment was just a case of careful nursing and keeping the patient as cool as possible whilst the fever lasted. I remember that my aunt Annie, who nursed several sufferers, often through the night, always waited for the crisis point when the fever would break and the patient would hopefully recover. Sadly, Rosa did not recover. It was a great loss and sadness to all who knew her and the whole village mourned her passing.

Mr. Morley was a very kind and friendly man and Mrs. Morley was equally so. I loved going to the farm where they always took pride in showing me the newborn animals. I used to go every Sunday to spend the day with them and, after dinner, Mrs. Morley would take my hand and we would go across the meadow to see all the animals. A special joy for me was when a new foal had been born and I could watch the mother and baby together. Mr. Morley often played games with me and I remember sitting on his lap and he would part his knees and I would fall through and he would lift me up and toss me in the air and sit me back on his lap, with much laughter from us all. I always visited them at Christmas and they kept a stocking for me, filled with presents. I was very lucky to have known such good people.

Mr and Mrs Morley

Little girls like new clothes and I was no exception so Elsie would take me to the big shops in Bury St Edmunds to buy my outfits. A new dress for the Anniversary, new dress for Christmas, a new outfit for summer and a new outfit for winter - these were strict instructions from dad to Elsie, to make sure I had what all the other girls had. Early in the morning, on the appointed shopping day, off I went on the bus with Elsie to buy my clothes. I remember that the bus conductor was very strict man and that I was quite frightened of him. The days of 'Have a Nice Day' had not arrived and little girls were expected to have the correct fare and to be no trouble. I was very glad to arrive at Bury St Edmunds without upsetting the conductor.

When we arrived, we would shop at Pretty's and Annette's, I remember, and I suffered excruciating embarrassment at Elsie's moans and groans because I could not bear any clothes that itched. I can hear her now saying to the shop girl that I was a 'daft little thing' for rejecting something that they thought was ideal for me. She did not suffer from this problem herself and was prone to exasperation at my apparent whims and fancies. And so we wended our merry way through the shops and by lunchtime we had selected most of my outfit. Lunch was the next thing and we carried our parcels up the stairs to the Co-op restaurant, where a waitress in a black dress with a white fancy apron and a white lace cap served us. Elsie would order a three-course meal for both of us and it all felt very grand. After lunch we finished our shopping and caught the bus back to Mildenhall where Freddie was waiting with his car to return us to West Row.

I could hardly wait to show mum and dad my new clothes and I tried all the things on we had bought for their approval. I did the same for my brothers when they came home and then carefully placed them in the drawers and wardrobe all ready for wearing.

Elsie with Una (seated in car)

Freddie Taylor Balls - my sister's husband: and (right) his first lorry

Elsie's new husband was, as I have mentioned before, quite an entrepreneur. He purchased the first of what was later to become a fleet of Lorries in which he transported locally grown flowers to Covent Garden in London. He was also a keen sportsman and competitor and had many trophies arranged on his sideboard. He played football in the winter, bowls in the summer and, in the shooting season; he attended as many of the local shoots as he could. He kept gun dogs and I remember one of them, named Tarzan, would gently take my hand in his mouth and lead me to the door, when I was visiting. It was amazing how soft his mouth was and showed how well he had been trained to pick up game.

The left-hand cottage was Elsie and Fred's first home in Thistley Green, next-door lived Mr. Frost (the butcher) and his family

Freddie was a tall fair-headed young man who, in addition to being quite good looking, was very even-tempered – this resulted in him being a very popular man in the village, with many friends. He was easy to get along with and was very kind to me when I was staying with them – he never seemed to mind me being there and always made me feel welcome. A great fan of cowboy books, he became convinced that I was also a fan and passed his large collection on to me. I consequently almost became a fan myself, becoming an avid reader of The Wild West, the Wagon Trains and tales of the Prairie Rose – as one of the heroines of many books was so aptly named. After I had read them we discussed them and decided which we enjoyed the most.

My brother Alec

My sister Elsie was around two years older than Alec and he was thus quite 'grown up' when I was born. I really did not see very much of him because he left home to join the Army, when he was but nineteen.   He enlisted in the Royal Artillery Regiment in 1931 and I really saw little more of him, except when he came on leave. I remember him as very nice young man, who had me in stitches, with his stories of Army life and of his mimicry of his Sergeant Major – who, it seemed, was a bit of a tyrant and who had him presenting arms with a broomstick, instead of a rifle and drilling the platoon endlessly. I thought him very handsome in his uniform and I felt very proud of him. He wrote me long letters of his adventures, which I treasured. He intended to make the army a career, however, and, although I saw little of him, I was very fond of him and always remained very close.

Brother Alec with an army friend

CHAPTER 6

Aunt Annie, Aunt Kate & Uncle Sid

Uncle Sid and Aunt Annie

My mother's two sisters Annie and Kate lived in the village. Annie was married to Sydney Bell and Kate was a spinster and an invalid who was cared for, all her life, by Annie. Sydney Bell farmed a smallholding on the Fifty Drove, which lay on the boundary of the village and the fens. He was of course my uncle and everyone that I knew called him uncle Sid - he was a lovely, fun-loving man, who played all kinds of jokes on all who came down to Fifty Farm.

I well remember, on Sunday afternoons, going into the small dairy where aunt Annie was separating the milk from the cream, using a very noisy and primitive hand separator. I used to take a small jug and fill it with cream from the spout. With a fork I then beat it until it thickened – taking great care not to spill any of the delicious cream (Aunt Annie was fastidious about cleanliness in the dairy).

I would take the thick cream into the kitchen to put on the jam tarts that aunt Annie had made in the morning. Aunt Annie had two children, a boy and a girl named Arthur and Mary, who were both older than me. We were very good friends and I loved them both very much. Mary and I would lay the table for tea - never knowing until the last moment how many places to set because aunt Annie's farm was open house for all to share. I, being the smallest, would sit next to uncle Sid, who always played one particular joke on me - which I always fell for. I had a habit of leaving the jam and cream of the tart until last, eating the pastry surround first. Uncle Sid always chose this moment to attract my attention to a visitor or some happening in the garden. I always looked to see who or what it was and, as I did so, he took my best bit of tart, and ate it in one enormous mouthful.

Uncle Sid always professed complete innocence and denied that he had any part of this ghastly deed but, after being chastised by aunt Annie, she would find another one for me. I am still careful not to leave the best mouthful until last, just in case he is still watching.

The farm was a delight for me with chickens, pigs, Bonzo the dog, a goat grazing on the drove, a cow for the milk and cats, but the only thing to mar my complete enjoyment were the geese. The boys used to tease them and they would chase me with their necks out straight and hissing like a steam boiler and I was frightened, really frightened. In the end uncle Sid made sure that the geese were penned when I was there. My dislike of geese is with me until this day.

Aunt Annie

My aunt Annie was a wonderful woman, a fact that was recognised by all who knew her. She was generous to a fault and a good friend to many who had fallen on hard times. She was also one of those precious people who helped to care for the sick in their greatest time of need and was able to nurse the terminally ill person in such a way that they were given peace and security – quite how is almost impossible to describe – but the nearest I can evoke is - like having an angel at the bedside. The inscription on her gravestone reads 'she lived her life for others' which was so true - she looked after her father and her crippled sister Kate, my cousins James and Reginald, my brother Don and any waif and stray who happened to appear on her doorstep and who was never turned away. I spent much of my childhood under her care and she always made me feel that I was very special. I am sure she made so many children and adults feel the same - she was, all her life a 'Good Samaritan.'

Aunt Annie and Aunt Kate

Aunt Kate

My aunt Kate, Annie's sister was crippled by tuberculosis from an early age. At one time she was confined (by her doctor) to a spinal carriage and to living in a specially fitted out shed in the garden - it was then considered to help with the treatment of the disease to live in a cold environment with plenty of fresh air.

In fact, aunt Kate recovered sufficiently to be able to walk with the aid of crutches. She also had a wheel chair which, needless to say, was completely fascinating to me. I could ride along with Kate when she was pushed around the village and feed on her never ending supply of sweets. The chair itself was made of wicker, as was the fashion in those days, and aunt Kate could steer the small front wheel, with a long wrought iron steering handle with a wooden extension in her lap. She felt the cold quite badly and was obliged to wear woollen gloves and a knee rug, in bright colours. Of course, I had to wear gloves as well to be like her.

Cousin Mary, Aunt Kate, cousin Dorothy, Jane Abrey and cousin Arthur

Aunt Kate was a very patient woman, particularly with children, and her long illness had not left her embittered in any way. Her one fear was that she would be left alone and wind up in the Workhouse, but Annie's care ensured that this would never happen and Kate lived for many years until passing away in the arms of her family.

Aunt Kate in later years

Influenza

In the early Thirties, an epidemic of influenza struck the inhabitants of West Row and the surrounding villages. Many deaths occurred and Mr. Aves, the gravedigger, was probably the busiest man for miles around. My father, on one of his visits to place flowers on the family graves, met him and remarked that he seemed very busy. Mr. Aves told him that on that morning he was allocating places for the graves to be dug and that he had just allocated a good spot for Mr. George Morley, alongside the graveyard wall. My dad was shocked by this news because George was a good friend of his and he had had no idea that he was so ill. However, he agreed that the allocated spot, by the wall, was an excellent one and he headed for home and lunch.

On the way home he ran into my brother Vic, who was also sorry to hear the news of George's expected demise. Vic, in turn, offered his condolences to Doodly,[5] George's brother, who worked for him. Doodly, too was most dismayed, especially as the last time he had seen his brother, he seemed to be recovering. He asked Vic for the afternoon off in order to call on his brother to make sure that he was still alive and Vic, of course, agreed.

---

[5] 'Doodly' was a nickname we all knew him as – I still don't know his real Christian name.

Doodly duly hurried off on his bicycle but in his own words,

> "Were 'mazed to find brother George sittin' up eatin' home made beef broth an' much better."

When George was finally up and about, Doodly told him what had happened and how Vic had - "scared im half to Death".

George charged off to confront Mr. Aves, who knew nothing of all this, and strenuously denied any wrongdoing. After some while it was all cleared up between them, although I understand some harsh words were exchanged and that George had said,"by the look of you Jack Aves I shall probably see YOU out" - which was his parting shot. Later they had a good laugh about all this and remained good friends for the rest of their lives.

This was a bad time as the Influenza Virus spread the disease through the village very quickly. The elderly and frail were the first to fall victim and even the young and strong were not immune to its infection. It was said that it was as if the plague had hit the area for there were funerals every few days. However it slowly passed, thanks to the care of the Doctors and the nursing by Nurse Butcher and the families of the ill. Spring arrived and with it the influenza vanished and all was calm and peaceful again.

CHAPTER 7

THE CLUB MONEY

These were the days before the National Health Service and people paid for their doctor's services privately. This was organised by the local doctors who ran a scheme called 'The Panel.' Families joined and made quarterly contributions, which enabled them to have full hospital and medical care at no further charge. In our family, it was my job to take the payment card and the money to Miss Fendick at the Manse. She duly signed the card and took the money - I did this every quarter. This scheme gave great peace of mind to my dad and he made sure that it was always paid on time. I knew that I must be careful with the card and money and to bring back the card duly receipted.

The Manse

I also took payment to the Shepherd Club that was paid to a Mr. Reeve every month. The Shepherd Club was an organisation set up to help working men if they fell sick, or out of work and to help with funeral expenses. Dad also paid into the Slate Club, which was slightly different in that the money collected from subscriptions was pooled and, after paying out to people in need (including funeral expenses), any unused funds at the end of the year, were shared out amongst the contributors, at Christmas. Generally this would be in the region of £1 – which would represent about two thirds of a working man's weekly wage and was thus quite a large sum to receive. Dad usually bought a stone of beef at Christmas with this money.

At this time it was considered a disgrace not to be able to afford a funeral for one's relatives and people were very conscious that they would be consigned to a pauper's grave if provision were not made for their funerals. At funerals it would not be seen as unusual for the Chairmen of both the Shepherd and Slate Clubs to walk in front of the coffin en route to the Chapel or Church. They would be dressed in black with a top hat, a black satin sash over one shoulder and carrying either a crook (for the Shepherd Club) or a bowler hat, and walking stick (for the Slate Club). I really felt part of it all because I had carried money to pay the dues each month. I was good friends with these serious gentlemen who always found a sweet for me before I left.

CHAPTER 8

DELIVERIES

Mr. Arthur Hinds owned one of the General Stores in the village. This was established in Friday Street which was not far from our house. It was a large double fronted shop with the door in the middle of two quite large windows. When you pushed to open the door a bell rang and you were immediately in an emporium of lovely things. Firstly, were the gorgeous smells of cured ham, bacon, cheese, intermingling with the odours of soaps, soda, candles and all manner of goods. There were long counters on each side: Groceries to the left hand and Clothes, and General Hardware to the right.

An early picture of Hinds' Store

Everything sold in those days was unwrapped, hence the lovely smells and to me it was like Aladdin's Cave, with so many wonderful things to buy. Of course all the goods sold had to be weighed, measured or prepared in some way. I can remember the sugar being weighed and then poured into blue bags, tea into red bags, and biscuits etc into white bags, all with the name A W Hinds emblazoned on the side.

Butter was cut from large blocks, which rested on the counter and then weighed and smoothed into shape with wooden butter pats. Cheese was very popular too - no choice, just Cheddar, also cut into large wedges and wrapped in greaseproof paper. Altogether a wonderful shop with the added bonus that Mr. Hinds came to the house, took the order and then his delivery boy would bring the goods the very next day. It was a sort of Tesco's home delivery service - only better because it was free.

I remember Mr. Hinds' name for Tizer was 'wind and water' which always made me giggle, and so much so that we nicknamed his delivery boy, Tizer. I believe just about everyone in the village adopted this nickname. So, Tizer brought the goods, carrying them in an enormous basket on the front of his delivery bicycle with A W Hinds painted on a panel between the frames. Tizer was a tall gangly youth who pedalled furiously round the village, whistling as he went and with a cheery word for everyone.

One day I saw a lovely doll in Mr. Hinds' shop and I asked dad if he would buy it for me. He replied that he was sorry but he could not afford it and that I would have to wait until his 'ship came in'. I made a point, from then on, every day to go down to the ferry to see if the ship was in. There was a small quay, close by the Ferry Public House, where barges would unload coal they had transported from Kings Lynn. I was thrilled a few weeks later when a larger ship than usual tied up at the quay and I was convinced that dad's ship had arrived. I raced home to tell him - only to be told that it was not the right ship but not to despair because it might come in one day. I never saw it come in but, later on, it must have arrived because at Christmas, in a box, there was the beautiful doll amongst my presents. I think the whole family must have shared in the joy of this moment with me, for I was so delighted.

My sister shopped at Whitworth Stores in Mildenhall and Mr. Wilbond, their salesman used to cycle up from Mildenhall each week to take her order. This may seem strange to modern women but it was the way it was done in those far off days.

Mr. Wilbond was a tall, dapper man, always in tweeds and wearing a trilby hat and bicycle clips, which he never removed, and which made him appear to be wearing plus-fours. He always came into my sister's kitchen for her order, entering it in a notebook, which he carried in a smart attaché case on the carrier of his bicycle. In the case were also details of any special offers and Mr. Wilbond, who was an expert salesman, suggested all kinds of goods for my sister to buy, which she couldn't possibly do without and which she had never thought of buying previously. Mr. Wilbond did this job for years and years, always on the same bicycle and, seemingly, in the same tweed suit. He was a truly happy man who was always cheerful and helpful. I had a great time once he had gone on his way because I also had a small case and a notebook standing by. I had also memorised some of his patter and was determined to sell my sister and her friends some great bargains and write their orders into my book.

Whitworth's motor-van delivered Elsie's order in the due course of time and I often helped her to put everything away in her various cupboards and stores. I found this a tedious task and I still feel just the same - I would much rather someone else put the shopping away.

We had a delivery of fruit each week from a real character - who was known throughout the area as 'Banana Bob.' He made all his deliveries riding a 3-wheeled tricycle of giant proportions. It had, however, an extra small front wheel so that a large container could be carried above it. In the container was his stock in trade, bananas, oranges, apples and pears and, in season, plums. Where they came from I'm not sure but they were always fresh and of good quality – he probably had fruit delivered by road from either Norwich or London. His rounds, took him to Mildenhall, West Row, Beck Row and Worlington with a starting point at Barton Mills on the main London to Norwich road. He ran a really successful business, calling at each village on a particular day of the week. Come rain or shine, he never failed us and was full of fun as he joked and laughed with everyone as he passed along.

He wore a light khaki full-length canvas coat, a chequered cap and black leather boots (if it was fine); if it rained, a yellow cape, sou'wester and leggings, bur he never missed a day. He also never missed his pint of beer at lunchtime and always vanished into The Plough. This was a signal for my brothers Leslie, Don and me to try and ride his tricycle, which he left, temptingly, in the yard of the pub. This was not as easy as we thought because the tricycle was very difficult to steer in a straight line - we always ended up riding round in circles.

I was always the passenger, sitting on the carrier, which contained the fruit and I used to fall off many times as they ran into posts and things. Little did we know that Bob was watching us from the pub window and, when he was suitably refreshed, he would appear shouting, shaking his fists and running to catch us. We always managed to elude him but I really think it was always a 'put up job' on his part. As long as we did no damage to his precious tricycle, he would enter into the fun of the occasion.

CHAPTER 9

THE OIL MAN

Billy Simpkins was our oil man. He was small in stature and wore glasses and a flat cap and a rather ancient black suit, which had suffered somewhat from the frequent spillage of paraffin. In fact he was so permeated by the spirit of his trade that, when he called at the house, we were always aware of that faint odour of paraffin. He was always happy and cheerful, however, and we all looked forward to his visits with great anticipation.

Billy used to call on us on Saturdays at around 6 o'clock in the evening. He owned a corner shop in West Street in Mildenhall, where he sold amongst a myriad of useful things, Sommerlite paraffin. Most important to us and to many in the surrounding villages, was that he also sold this from the back of his little van in which he called on us all in turn. It was only a small van but he had fitted a large tank at the back and he dispensed the paraffin into a gallon sized metal jug and then on into our containers. This was a real service to all the villagers for this was before the time of electricity and paraffin lamps were the only real illumination we had.

Billy had quite a business with his small van, for not only was he the oil man, but he also used to bring a large selection of household goods for sale. After filling our paraffin tank he would bring brooms, brushes, candles, soap, shoe polish, black lead polish for the grate, clothes pegs, and a host of other things too numerous to mention, into our living room. But I must mention the real treat for everyone was that he sold sweets from large tins in which were little bags of sweets (already measured and weighed) carrying labels saying 'Farthing', 'Halfpenny', 'Penny', 'Two Penny' and 'Three Penny'. From these tins the whole family chose their sweets for the week.

He certainly did well at our house for my sweet toothed elder brothers who were all working and had money to spend. My brother Don was still at school but, did odd jobs during the week, and so was able to buy his share of the goodies. Dad gave me pocket money each week so that I could join in the excitement and there was much fun. I can remember that my brother Vic always bought acid drops and kept them in his pocket with his red topped 'Bondman' tobacco tin. During the week he would share them with me and I can remember picking off the bits of tobacco before I popped one in my mouth.

It was not always smooth going, however, as sometimes we quarrelled over who should have what from Billy's tins but, he was a good mediator and with a twinkle in his eye, he would suggest an alternative and quickly settled the problem to our mutual satisfaction. He was a grand little man and his coming generated much noise and laughter and was the highlight of the weekend.

CHAPTER 10

WASHDAY

In one corner of the kitchen stood the copper with its own fireplace and chimney and, every Monday, my father lit the fire in the early morning. He then filled the copper with water from the well for our weekly wash. Washing in those days was hard work. There were no detergents or washing powders but only yellow cakes of soap and washing soda. Of course there were also no washing machines or spin driers. Large zinc baths were the norm for washing and rinsing.

Washday always progressed to a set routine. After the copper was heated some of the hot water was transferred to a zinc bath using a small wooden handled enamel pan. Cold water was added to the copper, which was left to boil, and more cold water was added so that the washing could be hand washed. Out came the scrubbing board and the clothes were scrubbed vigorously using Sunlight yellow soap on the metal board.

When satisfied that the washing was clean, it was wrung out by hand and placed in a dry tub ready for boiling. Washing soda was put in the copper together with the previously scrubbed clothes. The fire was built up and, when the water and the clothes were just boiling, cold water was splashed on the bubbles (from a jug kept handy by the copper's edge) in order to keep the copper from boiling over.

The washing was left to bubble away whilst we washed another bath full of clothes ready for the next boil. At this time the copper stick was produced. This was half a broom handle (supplied by the local shop) which, after much use, would become white from the regular immersion in boiling water and soap every wash day. Its main use was for stirring the clothes and was, I suppose, acting very much like today's agitator in a washing machine. It was also used for the somewhat hazardous chore of lifting the very hot clean washing from the copper into baths of cold water for rinsing - this was the tiring part.

Rinsing was backbreaking work. Firstly, three baths of cold water were required - this involved filling and carrying several heavy buckets from the well. The hot washing was then lifted into the first bath, wrung dry and then immersed in the second clean cold water bath. After wringing to get rid of any left over soapy water, coloured clothes were now ready for hanging on the linen line in the garden - wooden dolly pegs were used for this, which were supplied by the local gypsies.

The white washing, kept apart after the second rinse, was now dipped into the blue bath. This had been prepared earlier the same morning, whilst waiting for the copper to boil, by adding a 'Reckitts Blue Cube' wrapped in cloth and tied with string to a zinc bath full of cold water. The cube was swirled around in the water until it was judged to have reached the right colour. It was then removed and squeezed dry all ready for the next weeks wash day.

The Blue Bag also had a second use in that it was a very effective cure for wasp and bee stings. In the fruit season there were many blue spotted children and adults in the village. Why blue you may well ask? At sometime in the distant past I suppose someone had noticed that a pale blue dye had made cloth appear whiter and that dyers did not suffer with the effects of insect stings. Just plain serendipity I think!

Back to wash day..... The washing after its dip in the blue bath was hung out to dry after being wrung semi-dry by either hand or one of the new fangled mangles.[6] If the wash day had gone well, all the whites were now really white and blowing on the line. There was quite a competition to have the best looking line, and many a sniff about the results of a bad wash day.

There were heartbreaking days too, when it rained just as the washing was on the line, or the day when the line snapped and all the washing fell onto the muddy path. A woman's life was a hard one in those times, with much drudgery but, there was a real sense of accomplishment when the laborious task of washing had been completed. But it did not end there Tuesday was always ironing day.

In those days men wore stiffly starched collars, certainly on Sundays and often on high days and holidays. On workdays my family wore red and white spotted kerchiefs, which were knotted around the neck. On Sundays, their starched collars were fastened to the shirt by two collar studs. The stud at the back of the neck was a plain mushroom shaped stud but, the one at the front, was a pivoted one - to ensure that the collar was easy to fasten.

The real art of washday was washing and ironing the starched garments – for, besides collars for men, there were also starched pinafores, petticoats, and skirts for women, and lace tablecloths, doilies, table centres, antimacassars and sideboard runners for the home.

I thought you might like to know how we achieved such good results from a humble packet of starch as it is very little used nowadays and, before long I fear, it may become just one of those lost arts. First of all the starch we used was 'Robins' which we mixed with a small amount of cold water to form a smooth paste. When this was really smooth, boiling water was added and stirred until the mixture thickened into starch. Later, when it cooled, the clothes were dipped in the liquid and wrung out by hand and then put on the line to dry. All this happened after the main wash on Mondays.

On Tuesdays, the articles that had been 'starched' and dried the day before (hopefully!) were sprinkled with water, rolled up and left to dampen all the way through. The ironing was then done on the kitchen table covered by an old blanket and sheet and, when we were ready and the irons were hot, off we would go.

Electric irons were just not available to us, as there was no electricity in the village but our smooth flat irons were really superb. They were more difficult to use than the modern iron but the results were just as good. The temperature was calculated very simply: we just spat on the iron sole and, if it sizzled, it was hot enough. We kept things moving along by having two irons in operation. This is where the saying of having "several irons in the fire" comes from, I think. I would watch all this going on and looked forward to the time when I would be allowed to iron some simple things, such as pillowcases and tea-cloths.

We kept the iron clean by rubbing it with a cloth but, later on, a guard was invented to clip on the iron and so keep the sole clean. We would heat the iron as before but, instead of having to clean it each time, we clipped the guard to the iron and so protected the clothes.

The art of ironing starched collars and aprons is a difficult one to learn but the work had to be smooth and free from creases to satisfy the housewives in those far off days. It was deeply satisfying to see all the weekly wash ironed and folded ready to put away in the drawers.

---

[6] Not all households had mangles - many people did not see the need for them.

CHAPTER 11

FLOWERS AND THE FLOWER SHOW

After the end of the Great War farming in general fell into decline. The great stock market crash in America affected commodity prices in England and there was a general depression throughout Europe. Gradually things improved, although there was a dearth of young men to work on the land, because of the terrible losses in the Great War. I was born in 1928 and by the time I was approaching school age the recovery was well under way. A sugar beet factory was opened around this time and farmers began to plant the crop which offered them a regular income. Also the wonderful Covent Garden Market was selling flowers to Londoners, who bought all types of blooms and demanded more and more. The small-holders and farmers lost no opportunity in taking advantage of this newfound market and, in no time, people were growing flowers in abundance.

Flowers waiting to be packed

We grew Pyrethrums, Pinks, Poppies, Sweet Peas, Scabious, Sweet Sultan (both pink and yellow), Alstroemerias, Coreopsis, Geums, Anemones, Dahlias, Chrysanthemums, Statice and hosts of others. The flower season commenced in April and ended in October and, to take advantage of this trade, the whole village played a part.

Young girls picked flowers, mothers picked flowers, and grandmothers picked flowers and the men and boys too. Very quickly a whole new way of life started. Money was found to buy lorries to transport the flowers to London each day, where they would be auctioned to the London buyers. Flowers had to be in London by the very early hours of the morning and the empty boxes would be returned to West Row on the lorries homeward journey – ready for the next day's crop. The trade very quickly mushroomed and people in the village grew flowers on their allotments, back gardens and any space that could be found. The farmers also planted flowers, on fields where they had formerly grown cereals or vegetables. It was a real bonanza and many people became comfortably off from this 'stroke of luck.' My brother Don still has copies of invoices for flowers he sent to Covent Garden, whilst he was still at school. The motor lorries played a big part in this good fortune and, in fact, my sister's husband, Freddie Taylor-Balls, started a haulage company from owning just such a single lorry.

Freddie's first lorry

The flower pickers soon became proficient in gathering and bunching the flowers, which were tied with bass - a type of raffia. One could see them every day, picking the blooms, which were tied from the sheaf of bass at their waist, in dozens. They were carried to the end of the rows and then collected into the packing shed, where they were placed in buckets of water. Here they remained until they were packed into wooden boxes and wrapped in coloured tissue paper. Some of the more expensive blooms were arranged carefully and packed in cardboard boxes bearing the name of the flower wholesaler.

Flowers in boxes waiting for collection

The boxes of flowers were left at the front gate of the house or on the drove adjacent to the allotment. The lorries came in the evening to collect the boxes of flowers from all the growers (both large and small) and then set off for London at 10:00 pm, to be ready for the early morning market.

The Annual Flower Show & Thurston's Fair

The annual Flower Show was held in July on the second Thursday of the month. My Birthday is the 13th of July and I was born on Flower Show night so the Flower Show has a very special meaning for me. Quite when the Flower Show first started, I am not sure but I know that it was a big event in the life of the village.

There was also the Fair, which always arrived in the village at the same time as the Flower Show. There was great excitement when the Fair arrived. The large meadow behind the school was the venue for Thurston's Fair and it arrived behind a number of large steam engines towing dismantled roundabouts, dodgem cars, swings, stalls and all the accoutrements of a Fair. Places were eventually found in the meadow for all the equipment - amidst great clouds of steam, whistles, and much shouting (and some swearing) from the Fair people. By evening the whole meadow was ablaze with light and a cacophony of noise - my word this was an exciting time for both children and adults.

The Fairground staff seemed like athletic gods to the children and we watched, with open mouths, as those swarthy young men climbed over the roundabouts and swings, pulling ropes and tackles. The mighty steam engines that were smoking and hissing in the corner of the field, to supply the electricity to power all the lights and machinery, were constituents of an almost magical atmosphere.

The children were all given a holiday on the day of the Flower Show and this was an ideal time to use the school buildings to house the vast quantities of produce that was due to be displayed and judged. This meant the school had to be opened very early in the morning because competitors wanted to prepare their exhibits and displays. Everyone had a competitive streak and there was much talk and banter abounding on whom had the best produce and most artistic display. There was much competition amongst the ladies of course, and there were huge quantities of jam, pickles, cakes, sponges, scones and bread, all set out on the schoolroom trestle tables for judging by the visiting experts. Not to be left out, the children had their own display of handicrafts - including needlework, cookery, drawing and painting and there was also much competition between us to achieve a prize for our work.

On Thursday, the Flower Show day, we dressed in our Sunday best and our parents went down to the Show meadow for a final touch up of their exhibits – for by now the competition was becoming intense. The Judges arrived around 10:00 am, resplendent in blue suits and the occasional bowler and straw panama, and then the judging started in earnest. Prizes varied but mostly there were rosettes for 3rd and 2nd place and a larger rosette for 'Best in Class'. The ultimate prize was 'Best in Show' with a large bouquet for the winner.

Henry Bacon (seated on the special chair bought for him by the members of the Sunday School) with Mrs. Cook, Mrs. Fowler, Reverend Fowler and Mrs. Bacon before the sports and games began on Flower Show day

All the judging was completed by early afternoon when, with much excitement, all the children hurried to the school meadow for an afternoon of sports and games. The boys and girls took part in the three-legged race and the sack race and the egg and spoon race and lots of other fairly innocuous games. Then a children's edition of the tug-of-war with running races left until last. Soon it was time for tea and a chance to try some of those cakes and jams from the exhibition in the schoolhouse.

West Row Flower Show

At 5 o'clock the adult's games commenced with competitors from the neighbouring villages competing. My word! There was some competition between them, (with both the girls and the boys and the women and the men) and much shouting and cheering from all sides. The competitive games eventually ended with a final knock-out game of tug-of-war and the afternoon drew to a close with a flourish from a military band that had been playing all afternoon. I remember, on one occasion, we had the Black Watch Pipe Band who opened the Show with a march through the village from the War Memorial to the Show Ground. Another year we had the Dagenham Girl Pipers, who were a big attraction - especially for the boys.

With dusk falling it was time for the youngsters to be taken home as it was long past their bedtime. The Fair now came into its own, and the meadow was ablaze of lights and the music from the various fairground rides became louder and louder. The large roundabout (Jollity Farm) ran faster and faster and the Dodgem rides became shorter and shorter. The Fairground became packed with revellers and the excitement seemed to grow. The large swing boats, magnificent with their gaily-coloured stands, were great favourites and there was always a queue of people to ride in them. The men pulled hard on the coloured ropes trying to get the boats higher and higher. The girls screamed in case they went over the danger bar but, of course they never did, for even the strongest male was defeated by the weight of the boat and its occupants.

Jollity Farm

The festivities drew to a close around midnight and the steam engines slowed and finally stopped. All the lights went out and the machines lost their power. The music also faded and died and the meadow became empty, as the last of the revellers left for home. The Fairground quickly became a hive of industry with the crew's of the large machines dismantling the stands and all of the equipment - by morning they would be long gone and on to the next venue and another Fair.

CHAPTER 12

THE RIVER LARK

On summer days when the weather was warm, one of my favourite pastimes was a trip to the river. I would meet my friends at Bargate Farm and go through the farmyard with its many smells, and on down to the grassy riverbank. Bargate afforded a safe bathing place for all the village children - there was a slight bend in the river just there and the current was not strong. The water was shallow at the edge and was ideal for the little ones to paddle. As we grew older we would venture out to the middle, always making sure we could touch the bottom with our feet. Today, all children are taught to swim at school by law but, in those far off times, no such law existed. Somehow, we could all swim - some better than others, I suppose, but there seemed to be a competitive spirit in us all. The only aid we had was our brightly coloured inflatable rings, purchased from Mr. Hinds' shop in the village, which we used to help us learn to swim.

We would race each other to see who could swim against the current in the fastest time. The big thing was not to cheat by putting a foot down, either for a rest, or for a helpful push off the bottom. Bargate was an idyllic spot for children and grownups alike. Those long, hot summer days seemed to last for ever, swimming in the crystal-clear river, having picnics on the grassy bank beneath the trees, joining in the laughter and excitement - these must be treasured memories for the many children and parents who came along.

Judes Ferry and bridge (now replaced)

A few yards down stream from our bathing place lay Jude's Ferry. From time immemorial this had been a safe river crossing and had gone from a ford to a bridge many years before I was born. With the growth of religion in the area this spot was ideal for the Baptists to hold their Baptisms. The water was clean and shallow and it also was the site of the Jude's Ferry Inn which is still a flourishing Inn to this day.

Baptism is no longer carried out in the river but, in my childhood, it was a regular occurrence. Present day Baptisms are carried out in the Chapels but I think an immersion in a living river somehow seems to be more spiritual. There was always an impressive congregation from many of the surrounding villages when Baptisms were scheduled and a large crowd assembled on the bank. The minister, holding his prayer book and, accompanied by the deacons of the church, waded into the river to await the first person to be baptised.

Baptism at Judes Ferry

A deacon would bring the first woman, clad in a white cotton dress and white shoes, into the river and accompany her to the Minister. At this point the waiting congregation would sing 'Shall We Gather at the River' a rousing Baptist hymn always sung at these occasions. After a short prayer the Minister would hold her hands together as if in prayer and, with his other hand supporting her back, would lower her backwards so that she was completely immersed in the water.

After a few seconds he would lift her up, spluttering and coughing, with her white dress clinging to her and the accompanying deacon would escort her back to the riverbank. I am afraid that to a small girl only on the periphery of the ceremony, the religious message was lost on me, but I think my main feeling was one of concern to see the newly baptised leaving the river so bedraggled and wet. As I grew older, I learned that Baptism is a symbolic act of public witness to a personal faith, which already exists, and it does not cause the participator to become a Christian, it simply defines them as having already become one. This was a very real expression of faith because they were giving their future lives to Jesus and the Baptist Church. It was a great experience for them and a very joyous event for all involved.

Men were also baptised although, personally, I was not as concerned for their well- being. I think I thought at the time that they were more than able to look after themselves. I remember that one chap asked the minister if he could go face down as going backwards made him feel dizzy. His pleas went unheeded, however, and he was baptised in the usual way, suffering no ill effects, as far as I could see.

CHAPTER 13

HOLIDAY TIME

During the summer holiday from school I visited Dolly, my cousin, and her husband Percy at their small house in the next village, Beck Row. They lived right on the edge of the new aerodrome which was fast being constructed. I enjoyed myself immensely visiting my cousins who, incidentally, I called 'aunt and uncle.' They were so much older than me and I did not feel comfortable calling them by their Christian names.

Aunt Dolly and Uncle Percy on their Wedding Day

When the time came to pack my case I was very excited at the prospect of seeing them again and I chose the clothes I would require with some care - whether for best or for play. All my clothes had to be washed and ironed and packed ready for the big day and I would be ready to leave, long before the appointed time for Freddie's[7] car to arrive to pick me up and whisk me off to Beck Row.

---

[7] This was my Sister's husband Freddie Taylor Balls.

Aunt Dolly with her daughter, Thelma (who was born some years later) outside their cottage in Beck Row

I had such a warm welcome when I arrived at aunt Dolly and uncle Percy's house and spent the first afternoon unpacking my case, which I had so carefully packed the day before. My visit flew by, for we visited all the relations, went for long walks and picnics, and I quickly made new friends with the local children - every day we had new adventures. On Sunday we all went to the local Chapel but I really thought that our own Chapel in West Row was better - but these were thoughts of a little girl in a different place of worship, where things were not familiar.

Uncle Percy with my cousin Estelle (Topsy), in front of Mr. Ford's traction engine

Uncle Percy drove Mr. Ford's Traction Engine and the Threshing Machine, and was regarded by all as a very clever engineer. His working attire was some rather oily overalls and a flat black shiny cap - much smeared with oil and grease from the smoking monster that he tended and drove. At the time I was there, he worked regular hours but, in the busy time when he and his engine were in great demand, he worked from dawn to dusk. I used to wait at the gate for him to come home in the evenings, watching for his bicycle to appear in the distance. I was overjoyed to see him and his cheerful wave and I couldn't wait to tell him all the happenings of my day, whilst he would listen with much patience and good humour. He must have been very tired for he worked long hours but he always had time for me and I felt that he was interested in all I was doing.

After he had finished chatting to me, uncle Percy would quickly go and wash and change his clothes, whilst I helped aunt Dolly to lay the table for tea. When he returned, very spic and span and looking very different in his home clothes, we would sit down together for our evening meal and listen to the account of his day. Aunt Dolly was very kind to me and helped me in so many ways. I could always talk to her of any of the little worries I had and she always found time and the right words to help with any problem. She was a genuinely nice person and I was very happy to be with her.

My brother Don missed me very much whilst I was away from home - I spent a great deal of time either staying with aunt Annie or my sister Elsie. This was because of my mother's illness, which meant that she was unable to look after me and, being so young, I could not care for myself. Don, who was my nearest brother, therefore didn't see me as much as he would have liked - a fact I had not realised until recently, when we talked of our childhood and he mentioned how much he had missed me.

My brother Don

I was always pleased to be home again and to be with dad and mum and my brothers, and of them playing board games with me on the dark winter evenings. We had a lot of fun together and dad was a marvellous father who ensured that we were all well cared for and happy together.

CHAPTER 14

HARVEST TIME

The Harvest was without doubt the busiest time of the farming year. During the hours of daylight and sometimes into twilight, if the weather was fine, every available horse, binder, and man was hard at work. Men would be scything, stacking, loading tumbrels, and all the hard manual work involved in transferring the growing corn from the fields to the farm yards. Work started at daybreak and if a new field of corn was to be harvested, the men would set to cutting the headlands. They would cut a swathe of corn all round the edges of the field to allow the horse drawn reaper into the field and enable it to turn at the corners.

Little girls were not allowed on the harvest fields when all this was going on, so please forgive me if my description is not exactly accurate. I was able to watch from a handy gateway, however, and saw the men collecting the sheaves of cut corn and stacking them in shocks for drying. Later they were collected and transported to the farmyard. This is when I could join in and I had a wonderful time riding the bumpy old tumbrel from the yard to the field and then riding back again with a full load, astride one of the mighty Suffolk Punches. I remember how broad their backs were and how I had to cling on to their harness for dear life, especially when we walked up the rutted droves.

We used to take a picnic to the harvest field at tea-time, so that the men did not lose valuable harvest time coming home for a meal. We had many hungry mouths to feed and it was enjoyable for us to all to eat together in the field. In fact there was a very special harvest cake, which the wives and sweethearts made and which was a great favourite[8]. I remember that tea was made on primus stoves and all sorts of sandwiches were handed around - homemade bread of course and fruit from the gardens and allotments as well.

My friend Peggy Bacon and I had great fun in the harvest field, playing in the shocks of drying corn. We made a small house with the sheaves and next door we made a shop, collecting all kinds of things to sell. Discarded cigarette packets were everywhere and we collected them, together with match boxes – we were always on the look-out for goods suitable to display. Of course, this game only lasted as long as the sheaves took to dry out. As soon as it was considered that the sheaves were ready to stack, the horse and cart came along and we had to dismantle our home and business, though it was great fun whilst it lasted. Nobody seemed to mind us playing in the corner of the field even though we were playing in the sheaves because, I suppose, the drying process continued quite unaffected by our little games.

---

[8] Recipe in appendix 1

Grandfather Stone

When all was 'gathered in', with the fields cleared and the sheaves safely stacked in the farmyard, the farmer provided a 'Horkey' for all the employees who worked on the farm. A 'Horkey' was a harvest supper by which the farmer could thank all the men and boys who had worked so hard in the harvest fields. My grandfather Stone would help with the preparations, being responsible for the long simmering of the beef and the pork, in large coppers, the day before the big event. This made large quantities of broth which was given to any woman who brought a jug to collect it. The broth was full of goodness and could be made into a nourishing meal for their families.

Mr. Jaggard's Horkey

The men and boys all dressed in their Sunday best with their boots polished would meet at the Pear Tree Public House, in the village. Where they would all sit down to a huge spread of beef, pork, broad beans and all kinds of vegetables in abundance. There were puddings of all kinds and pies in profusion. Homemade beer was also provided in some quantity and great was the merriment and song - or so I was told, because little girls were definitely not invited.

There was a great camaraderie amongst the workforce. For the harvest, to be a successful one, took good organisation and much teamwork. There was a wonderful feeling of a 'job well done' amongst all who had taken part. A photographer would come from Bury to record the occasion and the festivities went on into the evening, ending with a singsong. What a time they all had - I wish I could have been there.

CHAPTER 15

THE BRITISH LEGION

The British Legion always paraded on the 1st Sunday in August. Quite why they had chosen this date, I really can't say but at least the 1st Sunday in August was an easy one to remember. We broke up from school on the Friday before, and it was also the day before Bank Holiday Monday. The parade commenced at the school. At the front of the parade was the West Row Band. They were followed by Major Neeve, head of the local branch of the Legion and Mr. Mothersole, the headmaster of the West Row School; both were resplendent in black suits, bowler hats, walking sticks and their campaign medals. Closely following were contingents of the West Suffolk Regiments, bearing their standards, followed by many old soldiers who had served in the Great War.

The Band would set off in fine style followed by the parade and by the numerous onlookers who marched behind to a selection of wartime songs. Reaching the War Memorial on the Green, the procession was met by the C of E Vicar, the Baptist Pastor and local dignitaries from the surrounding area, who were all seated on a cart that was decorated with flags and banners from various regiments. A Service of Remembrance was held in honour of the many young men who had been killed in the Great War. The roll of honour was read and I always waited to hear the names of my two uncles, who I never knew. The Last Post was sounded and the parade dispersed feeling quite subdued, until the band marched back to the school to a rousing tune.

There are two things that stand out clearly in my memory – one is Miss Fanny Ingle, wearing her late brother's red Suffolk Regiment uniform jacket, throughout the service. She was very tall and the jacket fitted her well - she wore it with great pride. The other is Mrs. Daisy Mackender singing 'Abide with Me', she had a beautiful voice and her performance was a very poignant moment for all the families present. I am sure that they were comforted with the knowledge that their loved ones had not been forgotten. A similar Service of Remembrance was held, nationally, on the Sunday closest to the 11th November Armistice Day. The service in West Row, however, was particularly for the local men who had failed to return to their families and so seemed more important to the community. I think it also shows how close local people were and how much everyone shared in and grieved the loss of so many fine young men.

CHAPTER 16

THE HARVEST FESTIVAL

In the autumn of the year when all the harvest was gathered in, the Harvest Festival was held in the Baptist Chapel and just about everyone in the village came, regardless of denomination. It was, as in all Harvest Festivals, an opportunity for all growers and gardeners alike, to show their best produce. The Chapel quickly became full, almost to overflowing, with fruit and vegetables. Pride of place was given to many sheaves of corn and the bread that had been baked from it. I seem to remember, that some pumpkins were also in the display and that the whole Chapel was a blaze of colour. However, the overwhelming impression was the most wonderful smell of freshly harvested produce, which filled the building.

My dad picked his best vegetables and apples and my brothers and I carried them along to the Chapel to ensure pride of place. The Deacons and many village ladies were there, arranging the displays (but we made sure that dad's produce was well to the fore).

The Festival service took place on the next Sunday and we almost had to queue to obtain seats, despite the addition of forms from the Sunday School in the aisles. All the local preachers and clergy attended and gave thanks for an abundant harvest and we all raised the roof with our versions of the old favourite harvest hymns. It was quite a moving occasion, especially as the service ended with all the produce on display being removed to share with the poor and infirm in the village - any surplus being taken to the hospital at Bury St Edmunds.

CHAPTER 17

AUTUMN CONCERT

(In Mr. Ball's Barn)

The villagers always put on an entertainment in Mr. Balls' barn in the autumn. Quite why, I never found out, except that it was a tradition and they just did it. It seemed that almost everyone in the village could either sing, or dance or tell funny stories, recite poetry or play a musical instrument and, in addition, was perfectly prepared to stand up and perform in front of an audience. A stage was built in the barn, after being stripped of its usual store of farm implements and machinery. Forms and chairs were borrowed for the audience and paraffin storm lanterns were provided for lighting. A piano was borrowed from someone in the village and I seem to remember that Mr. Walter Butcher was co-opted into playing his piano accordion.

There were many rehearsals required before the one and only performance and it was not unusual, when entering Mr Hinds' shop, to find someone rehearsing their lines or practising a song, whilst waiting to be served. Good humour prevailed, however, despite the occasional delays, and everyone in the village seemed to be looking forward to the concert with great anticipation.

On the night of the performance the barn was quickly filled with people and it was a scramble to find a good seat. The concert commenced, by special request, with Dolph Bacon's rendering of 'She was as Biiiiiiiiiiiutiful as a Butterfly' more commonly known as Pretty Polly Perkins of Paddington Green. The resounding finale of this song was greeted with great applause, whistles and shouts of 'encore' - I didn't really know what this meant but I shouted it, nevertheless, and everyone cheered even louder. I felt very pleased for Mr. Bacon.

'Dolph' Bacon at my brother Vic's stall on Bury Market

Other performers followed in turn and I clapped and cheered them all - from poetry readings, piano playing, comedians and many singers. One of my favourites was Mrs. Daisy Mackender, who sang a selection of 'The Old Ballads,' with 'Wartime Songs' and 'Tunes from the Music Halls', as a grand finale. All this was marvellous and the thrill of it is still with me. I have loved the theatre all my life and, it is wonderful to recall, something as simple as a village concert, kindled my love of the arts.

CHAPTER 18

THE SEASON OF MELLOW FRUITFULNESS

Work did not stop with the corn harvest for the fruits and produce from gardens, allotments and hedgerows had to be collected and stored. There were apples and plums to pick along with blackberries from the hedgerows and mushrooms from the fields. Walnuts and chestnuts were gathered, as were tomatoes, onions and shallots. There were many tasks to do and many jobs for small hands too.

Apples, both cookers and eaters were picked and sorted for the best quality fruit, which were carefully stored on wooden shelves in the shed. These would last throughout the winter provided they were covered with sacks during the coldest part of the year. My job was to collect the 'windfalls' and to sort over the best of them for puddings and pies, to be used quickly and then to stack any damaged fruit to be fed to the pigs.

The plums, Early Rivers, Victoria, Damsons and Green Gages were picked and preserved in Kilner Jars, to be used in the winter. Eggs were generally in good supply at this time of the year because the hens would be laying well - any excess we put down for preserving - we always had a good supply of eggs for baking in the winter months. We put them into crockery jars or enamelled pails; we mixed the Isinglass with water and poured it over the eggs so they were completely covered. This was not my most enjoyable job as the mixture was thick and slimy and I disliked putting my hands in it. I should have used a spoon, of course, but hands were quicker and you didn't break the eggs. At this time, any unripened tomatoes still on the vine, were made into green tomato chutney. The chutney was lovely to eat when cooked and matured but it had a most unpleasant odour when being prepared - the whole kitchen would reek of hot vinegar and spices for hours.

My dad lifted the onions and shallots from the ground to dry in rows in the autumn sunshine. When the onions were ready to be stored for the winter, he would gather them up and tie them into bunches, which he would hang from the rafters in the shed. It was wonderful to go into his shed in the winter, with the lovely smell of the apples and onions, to choose a selection for our Sunday dinner. Shallots, on the other hand, were lifted and then brought into the house to be peeled and put into jars of vinegar and spices. They were then stored in the pantry for some 6 weeks to mature; these were a great favourite with cold meats.

Walnuts had a double harvest for the nuts, when first formed and still soft, would be picked and pickled in brown vinegar and assorted spices. The result of this would become a delicious black soft walnut very tasty with cold meats and cheese. The mature nuts were allowed to hang on the trees until the green outer skin started to split and then were picked. This required some skill for if too early the kernel would be small and soft, if too late the kernel would have a coarse brown skin, which was the very devil to remove when peeling them. Most of the children had brown fingers from the juice from the green skins at this time of the year but, the wonderful sweet taste of newly picked walnuts, was well worth all the trouble taken to pick them.

How times have changed, for nowadays we can buy fruit and vegetables all the year round and so many of the old skills have vanished. I am sure many of the young folk of today would throw up their hands in horror if they were asked to work as we did, to the season, rather than to the availability of food from the supermarkets, with the supplies from all over the world. I can only say that the old ways gave women a great deal of satisfaction and pride and I feel fortunate to have experienced some of the 'old times'. However, it does seem to me, that although the young women of today are free from some of the drudgery experienced by the housewives of the thirties, with full time jobs, caring for the children, running the older children to their various hobbies and pursuits and driving the people carriers in today's heavy traffic, I think that the role of women in family life today is just as hard and very much more stressful than in the past - they are much to be admired.

CHAPTER 19

THE AIR RACE

The whole village was alive with the news that the long talked of Air Race to Melbourne, Australia was to be started from the newly built aerodrome, at Mildenhall, which fringed West Row. The air race was to celebrate the centenary of Melbourne which occurred in October 1934. Initially, advertised as having 60 starters, this was soon whittled down to 30 - but I think in the end 20 aeroplanes actually took off on the great adventure. It turned out that the whole country became air race mad and the enthusiasm filtered down to West Row, in particular, once it was learned that it was to start just over the garden fence as it were.

The King and Queen on their visit to Mildenhall – Mr. & Mrs. Mollison are on the extreme right of this photograph (Photograph courtesy of Bury Free Press)

The newspapers had a field day listing the types and names of the aeroplanes entered and, most of all, the names of the airmen and women who would be making this epic voyage into the unknown. The most famous duo was Amy Johnson with her husband Jim Mollison, who had been the nation's heroes for some while, with their exploits in the air. They were firm favourites to win this challenging race. This was divided into 5 parts, with checkpoints at Baghdad, Allahabad, Singapore, Darwin, Charleville and finally Melbourne, a total of 11,300 miles from the start. I learnt all this from my brothers and sister who read the newspapers avidly and were looking forward with great excitement to the arrival of these daring aviators.

The Prince of Wales talking to C. Scott and T. Campbell Black (back to camera) the eventual winners of the race. (Photograph courtesy of Bury Free Press)

The date set for the start of the race was Oct 19th 1934 and, even though I was only six years old, I joined in with the excitement whenever I could. As the day of the race grew closer and the aeroplanes started to arrive, an area near the stationary aircraft was roped off and all the locals were invited to pay two shillings and six pence to watch them prepare for the race. Alternatively you could pay 5 shillings to meet the pilots and their crews - my brother Vic did just that. My sister was very annoyed because she had only bought the two shillings and sixpence ticket, not knowing about the 5 shilling one and let us all know her feelings when she came home. She soon recovered her good humour when my brother gave her a selection of postcards he had bought on the airfield, showing the planes and their pilots. He gave some to me as well, so we all had a share in his generosity.

As the race day came nearer, it became obvious that it had aroused far more interest than the organisers had allowed for. There was international interest too because there was a large contingent of Dutch people supporting their entrant in the race and 'hundreds of Indians and many Japanese'[9]. Very quickly all the local hotels and boarding houses became fully booked and not a bed was to be found anywhere. Vast crowds of viewers swamped the aerodrome and some of the competitors were complaining of damage to their aeroplanes. People were parking their cars in every available site in order to view the start of the race and slept overnight for several days beforehand, so as not to lose their spot.

It was estimated that by the evening of the start there were over 60,000 people at, in, or close to the airfield. Added to this were revellers coming by car from numerous parties held as far away as Cambridge. There was the unusual sight of men in dinner jackets and ladies in flimsy evening dresses, walking towards the aerodrome in the dark (having abandoned their cars miles away). I

---

[9] Bury Free Press, October 27th 1934, page 2.

heard it said that most of the main roads were jammed and all traffic was at a standstill and people were walking miles to get as close to the aerodrome as possible.

The aerodrome itself was brand new with several hangars and a large concrete apron on which the competitors' aeroplanes were standing. The Control Tower was between the hangars and there were 3 grass runways. The longest of these was NE to SW and was the runway designated for the race. The aeroplanes would be starting their take-off at 45 second intervals and the time of their take-off was to be sent by radio to Melbourne so that the times could be calculated at the end of the race.

The race was to start at 6.30 am and I was to be allowed to watch the take off and not miss all the excitement. We had all been promised a place on Mr. Aves' haystack, which afforded a clear and unobstructed view down the main runway. So, at around 5.00am, Dad awakened us all and we quickly dressed, had a bite to eat and trudged off across the farmyard. I was the only girl in the party of boys, who had been told in no uncertain terms by dad to look after me and this they did. I was carried to the top of the enormous stack with the aid of a ladder.

Once safely seated I watched the sunrise, probably for the first time in my life. We could already hear the sound of the aeroplane engines warming up and before long the first plane started to move - the boys told me that it was Amy and Jim Mollison. It had rained in the night and suddenly there was the most miraculous sight of a full rainbow at the end of the runway. The planes were all moving now because there was to be only 45 seconds between each take off and there was a cacophony of noise as they all readied themselves for their great adventure. One by one they all flew through the arch of the rainbow and we waved and cheered each one until they were all gone, which took only 15 minutes.

There followed an eerie silence as we descended from our vantage point. I think we all felt that we had witnessed something really special. Breakfast that morning was a great treat because dad had brought home 13 white herrings the previous evening to celebrate the occasion. They cost 1 shilling for 12 fish - but the fishmonger always gave dad an extra one for being a regular customer. My mother cooked them, rolled in flour and fried in lard in a large cast iron pan until their skins were golden brown and crispy. Served with freshly baked bread and butter they were a wonderful breakfast.

I was lucky that day for we had been given a day off school for the Air Race and I spent most of the time waving to the occupants of the hundreds of cars which were stranded in the traffic jams leaving the aerodrome. It was said that you could have easily walked from the aerodrome for miles on the roofs of the cars and it was really not until evening that things returned to normal again.

There is no doubt that the Air Race was a major event, which caught the imagination of many many people, including the Royal Family, who had visited the airfield the day before the start. The whole country was completely taken up with the outcome of the race, and, in particular, of the favourites Amy and Jim Mollison who had won the hearts of the nation. How strange all that excitement seems today, when air travel is so commonplace that the sight or sound of a jumbo jet passing overhead is hardly noticed.

We listened to the wireless for news of the race and followed the newspaper maps of the progress of the competitors with great interest. Our heroes, Amy and Jim, who were leading the race in their De Haviland Comet, Black Prince, alas, had to retire in India with engine trouble – however, to sweeten the pill, they had smashed the old record flight time (50 hours) by taking just 22 hours and thirteen minutes to reach the sub-continent. Even more sadly, two New Zealand pilots,

Flying Officer H D Gilman and Flight Lieutenant J K C Baines, lost their lives trying to land in southern Italy.

After an epic journey, however, the race was eventually won, in less than 72 hours, by C Scott and T Campbell Black in their DeHaviland Comet named and presumably sponsored by Grosvenor House. They claimed the first prize of £10,000 and were also in first place in the handicap but the rules prohibited them from claiming both prizes. The Handicap Prize was awarded to Moll and Parmentier, in a Douglas DC2, entered by KLM.

D.H. "COMET"

The following year a new cinema was built in Mildenhall and was named The Comet and it served the local population well, until its eventual demolition some fifty or so years later.

CHAPTER 20

THE SUGAR BEET

The sugar beet factory in Ely was in production before I was born. Farmers in the fens would grow sugar beet and, at harvest time, transport their crop to the river Lark in horse drawn tumbrels. There were several wooden loading chutes along the river – the furthest upstream being adjacent to Fifty Farm – where the sugar beet was tipped into waiting barges that could carry as much as 30 tons of beet per load to the factory at Ely for processing. However, because the barges could not navigate beyond Fifty Farm, there was no stimulus for farmers in and around West Row to grow sugar beet.

When the sugar beet factory was built in Bury St Edmunds a great change took place in our village. Previously grain had been grown but a few farmers, who were trying out this new crop, now planted the fields with sugar beet. The few quickly became the majority, when lorries became available to transport the crop cheaply to the factory and it was found that 'good money' was to be made. My dad rented a three-acre field from the Mildenhall Rural and District Council and, being cautious, grew half the field with barley and half with sugar beet. It soon became obvious that the returns were better from the sugar beet and, from then on, he grew only this crop.

The seed was planted in March and the beginning of April (no later than the 2nd week in April) using a hired, horse-drawn drill. When the seedlings had grown and the long lines of the new plants could be seen clearly, it was time for the 'chopping out' to be done - this entailed much work with a hoe whereby only clumps of the growing seedlings were left at about one-foot intervals. Following this there came the back breaking job of 'singling' which, as the name suggests, was the removing of all but a single plant and had to be done by hand.

This was really hard work and was generally undertaken by women and young folk and the pay was very good. Sacking was tied above and below each knee, using binder twine - this gave some protection from the stones, when crawling along the rows of sugar beet (with the plants between hands and knees). When I was older, I thought I would try this job with my cousin Mary, who had done this job before. We arranged with dad a price to single his field.

We started on the first fine day and I think early on my very first hands and knees trip up the first row, I realised that I had made a big mistake and that this was not for me - I really did not like the job at all. By the time I was at the end of the second row, with my back killing me, I vowed never to do this task again. When I looked at how much was still be done my heart sank - for 3 acres looks about 3 miles, when one is kneeling, pulling out plants, to leave one plant at 1 foot intervals.

The best part for me was the company of my cousin, Mary, and the sandwiches and cake provided by aunt Annie. She had given us what proved to be a lifesaver, in the form of bottles of cold cocoa, and we rewarded ourselves with a drink at the end of each row.

The job went on and on until eventually it was lunchtime, when we stopped for a whole hour and enjoyed the sandwiches and cake. Mary was a great help in lifting my spirits and we set off again and, at last, we came to the end few rows, in the late afternoon. I thought we would never finish - but all things come to an end, whether they are good or bad and, much to my surprise, we did eventually finish the whole field. I made a vow at this time that never, never, never would I go singling again - and I never did.

The sugar beet was left to grow throughout the summer months, with an occasional weeding which dad did with his hoe. The soil on his land was very good which guaranteed an excellent crop (depending on the weather of course). Around the end of September, the sugar beet crop was ready to lift and, as was common with all land work at this time (before mechanisation), lifting was very labour intensive.

In order that the beet could be lifted manually, a horse and single furrow plough was used to loosen the soil. When this had been done over the whole field, the next operation was commenced - which was called 'pull and chop' and involved my dad and some hired labour. Each man worked two rows at a time, pulling the beet in alternate rows by hand and knocking them together to free them from any soil. Then, using the beet hook that each man carried, the green top of each tuber was cut off and discarded. The remaining large root was left on the land to be collected by a horse and cart, which followed along later.

Two labourers ready to 'cut and chop' once the horse drawn plough had loosened the soil.

At this time a special six-tine fork was used which was similar to a garden fork but which had six tempered tines, with protective balls on the end (to prevent damaging the crop) and a deep bulbous shape. The beet was then loaded into the horse and cart and trundled off to the end of the field. It was unloaded into a pile, ready to be collected by a large lorry, which would transport it to the sugar beet factory at Bury St Edmunds, to be processed into sugar.

At the time of the harvesting of the beet, the roads around most fields and even the village streets were smothered with mud from the wheels of the lorries that carried the sugar beet. Woe betide a walker if it had rained - one could arrive at one's destination in a very sorry state.

I was very concerned at this time about my father's hands. Because of the very hard work involved and the cold weather, he suffered from deep cracks to his fingers. When I said I was worried, he told me not to fret as he had some magic ointment, which would cure them. Sure enough, after a few applications, the ointment did work magic and the cracks all healed over. I learned some years later, that the magic ointment was called 'Zambuc.' It was a thick, green jelly, which seemed to be a cure for all skin problems.

CHAPTER 21

STEAMING

Earlier I wrote about the harvesting of the ripe corn and the stacking of the sheaves in the farmyard. Now, around November, came the exciting time known as steaming – which was the final part of the harvesting process, when the dried corn was threshed, bagged and taken to the granary to await a visit from the corn merchant, to arrange a price.

The threshing machine in action, with the sacks of corn being filled (nearest to camera) and the straw (furthest from camera) ready to be elevated to the growing stack.

First of all, arrangements had to be made to hire the traction engine and driver and the threshing machine, on the best available date. The hiring of additional labour was also needed to ensure the whole event went without a hitch. The work involved was heavy, dangerous and dirty and, as a result, high wages were paid – around a shilling an hour for the best men. Steaming, although partly mechanised, remained a labour intensive activity. The work involved taking the sheaves from the stacks to the threshing machine, splitting up the sheaves and feeding the corn into the machine, lifting the sacked corn weighing one comb (16 stones) on to a cart and hence to the granary and of course the one hundred and one jobs involved by all this.

On the appointed day, first thing in the morning, a line of men would appear at the farmyard, and the farmer or his foreman would choose the men required. My dad did this work and he was always chosen because the local farmers and their foreman were aware of his reputation as a reliable worker. Then, amidst a great deal of noise, smoke, steam and shouting, the traction engine would arrive towing the threshing machine. After much manoeuvring the whole contraption was shunted into place and things were almost ready to commence. I was definitely not allowed near the farmyard when the engine arrived but I would watch it being driven up the village street with a great rattling and puffing noise and I would look to see if my uncle Percy was driving it. I would wave and blow kisses to him and he would doff his engineer's cap to me and wave - much to my delight.

Steaming – the whole process: steam engine, threshing machine and stack

The time involved for the steaming was all according to the size of the farm but the end result was that all the corn was threshed before the engine and threshing machine moved off to the next farm and the grain had been stored in the farm granary. If the men taking part could have known that all the hard work, including cutting the corn and threshing would be carried out by one man and a combine harvester and the bags of grain taken to the granary the same day, they would have thought it impossible.

Job done: the photograph shows the neatly thatched haystacks

CHAPTER 22

SHOOTING

Most of the men in West Row owned a gun and, in the wintertime, it was a common sight to see a group of men, walking across the fields in search of game. Whatever was shot was shared out amongst the villagers and this was a great help for the housewife. To be given a pheasant or a brace of partridges, which made a splendid dinner, was an excellent gift and much appreciated by all who received them.

Billy Webb, Russell Clarke, George Bloom, Raymond Rolfe, Ralph Reeve, Fred Taylor Balls and a beater

Some women learned how to pluck and draw game and my sister was very proficient at this. She could prepare a pheasant for the oven very quickly - I, on the other hand, had no talent for this job and, could not even watch it being done. A pheasant made a tasty meal and with home made stuffing, rich gravy and home grown vegetables, was very good.

When Elsie was preparing game, I was banished to the washing up bowl - which I didn't really mind as I felt that almost anything was better than plucking a pheasant. I had similar troubles with rabbits - but thankfully Elsie was good at those too and could skin a rabbit in a trice - which was lucky for me as we ate lots of rabbits. A great favourite with us all was rabbit pie, which made a very tasty meal. Rabbits, long before myxomatosis, were in abundance in all the fields and so were readily available.

On Boxing Day it was a tradition for anyone who owned a gun to walk the fens in search of game. It was also a tradition to have a few drinks when the shooting was over at the local pub, where a meal was also provided for the 'guns'. Any surplus birds or rabbits would be sold to the local butchers and everyone had a very merry time (I was told). The day after Boxing Day was a very quiet one and for some reason, I found that few seemed to be ready for a walk.

CHAPTER 23

DYKING

There was little work on the farms in the winter months - indeed, winters then seemed to be much more severe and longer than in the present day. My dad found work in the fens on the maintenance of the banks, sluices and drains. I think the pay was good and the hours were short - because work could only be undertaken in daylight. This job was called Dyking which was obviously a word left behind by the original Dutch drainers of the Fens. The work consisted of clearing the waterways of the accumulated weeds, reeds and the mud, which had been washed from the land - this mud was as black as coal and dad used to come home looking like a coalman.

The soil in the fens was, despite its appearance, a light one and in the spring with the March winds, the whole fen would start to 'blow'. This was when the black earth would be blown several hundred feet in the air and the countryside would be engulfed in a black cloud. I was told that it was similar to a sandstorm in the desert because, when it occurred, we all had to keep our windows and doors firmly closed. It seemed to get in everywhere despite our house being quite a few miles from the fen itself. The fen blows were quite a problem too, for not only was the rich topsoil blown away but the valuable seedbed of any newly germinated crops. Farmers would often have to replant whole fields.

Of course the men working at 'Dyking' had to take their own food and drink and this was prepared for dad before he left on the transport to the fen. This meant that one of us had to pack his cheese and pickles and plenty of bread, together with slices of home made cake and two bottles of cold tea, in Tizer bottles.

My father (with pipe) working on the dykes

A real bonus of my dad working on the dykes was the abundance of eels. Dad used to catch them using his eel fork - a flat bladed five-pronged tool specially made to trap the eels just behind their heads. He would pull the eels out of the reeds with the fork and quickly drop them into a pail carried especially for the job. At the end of the day he brought them home, skinned them and cut them into small pieces. Mum then poached them in a large frying pan and served them in a melted butter sauce[10]. They were delicious served with a large hunk of home made bread, which we dipped in the sauce.

There were no bones in the eels and they were a favourite treat for us all. There was one problem which dad had to get round, however, and this was me. I had to be kept out of the way when he arrived with his eel pail because I hated the sight of those live wriggling writhing and slimy eels. Dad made sure that the first sight I had of them was skinned and in the pan.

Dyking lasted only over the winter months and then dad returned to general farm work. There were no more eels until the next winter. I can still remember how marvellous they were. Imagine, eels eaten within a few hours of being caught - try them if you can.

---

[10] Melted Butter Sauce is what is now known as 'White Sauce' – made with corn-flour, butter and milk.

CHAPTER 23

TELEPHONE AND ELECTRICITY

An exiting day was when the Post Office men arrived to install a telephone service in the village. I had heard talk of its coming but wasn't really sure what it was or how it was arriving. I was delighted when lorries with long poles and great drums of wire drew onto the green. Large athletic men were soon busy digging holes all over the place. Very quickly poles were erected in the holes and even more athletic men were climbing the poles and connecting wires to some of the houses. The first telephone box in the village appeared, as if by magic, near the church and a second beside the well pond at the other end of the village. We could hardly believe that we had telephones and were now connected to the outside world.

My brothers Don and Leslie were fascinated by all this and decided to have their own telephone system - having read in their comics that you could make a telephone from two tin cans and a length of string. They selected two trees in our garden and, using a roll of binder twine, discovered in dad's shed, they proceeded to construct their own West Row telephone system. I was conscripted to search for two leather belts (also from dad's shed) and two bags for tools, which they planned to carry around their waists – just as the men from the Post Office had done. I was not allowed to participate in the great scheme, beyond searching for things, and was expressly forbidden to climb the trees by the two budding telephone engineers.

Up they climbed using the belts for safety and perched, each one, on their individual tree. Down came the binder twine from Don's tree and I was instructed to take it over to Leslie's tree and to tie it onto his length of twine (which he had dangled down from his tree). Here they met with a snag - I didn't do knots. This caused some consternation amongst the 'engineers' and resulted in much abuse coming from the tree-tops. Brother Don eventually had to climb down, tie the twines together and climb back up. Why he did not carry the twine up the tree in the first place, was beyond me, but I dared not ask him for fear of not being allowed to join in further.

Anyway, they begrudgingly let me go on helping, especially when they remembered that a hole had to be cut in the bottom of each tin and that they needed a knife. Leslie came down this time, much put out and blaming me for forgetting it. He sent me off post haste to find one - which took me some while because I could not find the one he wanted. At last I did find the elusive knife and I carried it back triumphantly, only to find that Don had had a penknife in his pocket all the time. Oh dear I was in the wrong again but I still couldn't understand why.

They finally connected the cans together and, joy - it worked! They were able to talk together but, in my innocence, I said it was such a short distance between the two trees that it would have been easier to shout to each other. I was told to shut up and not to be so stupid - they were talking on the phone.

I was very anxious to be a complete partner in this venture and to be able to climb the trees with them and talk on the cans (phones). They would not even consider it because, apparently, girls don't climb trees. However, a compromise was reached. After a very long and tearful argument from me, I was permitted to use their highly technical equipment at ground level. I was learning feminine wiles at an early age, you see.

Electricity

The next major event was 'the coming of the electricity' which was to be provided by the East Anglian Electric Light Company based at Mildenhall. This caused some concern in the village because not everyone could afford the cost. In addition, some people could not see the advantage of having it at all - they had been perfectly happy for years with their oil lamps and solid fuel cookers. Really, the main objection was the cost, which was the sum of £9.00 for the installation of one electric socket (15 amp) and three lights. A working man's wage was around 30 shillings per week at this time, so it was no wonder that many people just could not afford to take advantage of the opportunity to 'go on the electric'.

Despite the objections, it was not long before the poles were installed all over the village. Slowly the advantages were realised and the objectors were won over. My dad was involved in the erection of the poles throughout the village and they are still standing today, some 76 years later. After the poles were erected it was not long before the streetlights were installed. What a joy it was to be able to walk along the lighted streets, without having to carry a torch or lantern to light one's way. At home, we were not one of the lucky few to have the electricity connected right away and still used the oil lamps and candles. As I was a great reader I was allowed to read in bed by candle light with frequent admonishments from dad who was worried in case I strained my eyes. He was no doubt protecting me but, at the time, I felt really 'hard done by' in not being allowed to finish my chapter.

CHAPTER 24

My Mother holding Vic, in 1910

Mother wore her hair short. She had long slender fingers and kept her nails well manicured and she was always neatly dressed – often in a pinafore, as was the fashion of the day.   I am not sure quite when she first became ill but it was sometime shortly after I was born. Her illness manifested itself in an almost complete withdrawal into a world of her own. She was able to communicate with us but had changed, from a lively intelligent woman, who was actively involved in events in the village, to a person who rarely spoke and became distressed and disturbed whenever anybody called at the house. Even her sisters were unable to visit us and, in consequence, she became increasingly more isolated from the outside world.

Despite her illness, my mother was quite able to undertake all the household chores - such as washing and ironing and she was also a good cook – baking cakes, making jam and bottling fruit, in season. Her meals were delicious and were always on time but were produced in complete silence. Being so young, I knew nothing of my mother's illness at the time or of the great strain it put upon my father – who had to cope with me, as an infant child, my brother Don (who was three years my senior), my brother Leslie, who was still at school and my sister Elsie, who was 16. There was also my elder brother Victor, who lived with us – we were quite a large family.

In these early days, I was cared for by my sister Elsie and, occasionally, by my aunt Annie – who would look after me if I were unwell.[11] I often spent time with her and uncle Sid, at their small cottage opposite the Well pond in the village[12], much to my sister Elsie's relief I am sure.

As I became older, I realised that my mother was not as my friends' mothers were and, although not violent or unkind, she would not talk to anyone and avoided contact with the outside world. There were a few exceptions – she seemed to recognise Billy Simkins the oilman and also Mr. Hinds with the groceries. I felt a great sadness that she had to endure this affliction and tried, even at an early age, to protect her.

There were times when my mother seemed to be in some distress and it was then that she would talk to herself and appear to be troubled. Most of the time, however, she was at ease and watched my brother and I at play with a loving smile on her face. She liked, in particular, for us to play with the crayon box and we would give her a crayon to hold and she would pretend to draw and then would smile with pleasure.

Mental illness was a 'taboo subject' in those days and was not discussed in front of the children. It was thus little wonder then that we failed to understand my mother's illness or what was happening. Mental patients, at that time, were also often committed to Asylums for the Insane and many families would live in fear that this would happen. The response was that patients' families would often 'close ranks' in order to protect loved ones and to ensure that, whenever possible, outsiders new nothing of their troubles.

My brother Don and I both loved our mother dearly and in some strange way we were able to bond with her. Both of us have happy memories of the times we spent together. The only real regret we have is that, unlike our older siblings, we never knew her when she was well - she must have been a lovely person. There were odd times when she surprised us all, however, and one particular occasion I remember very well. We were all engaged in a family crossword puzzle and were completely confounded by an obscure clue, when my mother, who had been sitting silently by the fire, suddenly came up with the answer and the correct spelling. We all looked at her in amazement but she just smiled a little smile and returned to her silence.

Not all my memories of my mother are sad ones because she seemed to love many things – the flowers my brother Vic brought her each week are a good example. She would smile with pleasure when he brought them home and bustle about arranging them in different vases about the house. Clothes too gave her immense pleasure and she would spend hours brushing them and re-arranging them in her wardrobe.

My mother would, very occasionally, when she was left on her own, go for a walk. She would dress in her best clothes and, wearing her favourite hat, would set off around the village and then head on to Mildenhall – which always seemed to be favoured destination[13]. She spoke to no one on her journey, just walked quietly along. When dad and the boys came home and found her missing there was great consternation and everyone set off in different directions to try and find her. When she was found – and she always was – she would just smile and walk home with whoever had found her. She would then put her clothes and hat away and then carry on as if nothing had happened. We were all very relieved when she arrived home safe and well and still smiling gently.

---

[11] Aunt Annie said later that I walked, for the first time, on one of these occasions.
[12] Aunt Annie and Uncle Sid lived in this cottage before moving to Fifty Farm.
[13] We were never able to discover why she walked to Mildenhall.

My settled life at home was changed again, when Freddie, who had been courting my sister Elsie for some while, asked my father for her hand in marriage. This was to present him with a major problem because I was only five years old at the time and, if Elsie left home, as she surely would, there was no one to look after me. Aunt Annie came to the rescue, as she always did, and it was arranged that I would live with her and her family for a while and only return home for visits. So I became one more member of my aunt Annie's family who, together with uncle Sid, treated me with love and affection.

I missed my mother and family very much but the love I was given helped me to overcome being away from home. My brother Don visited me as much as he could because I know he felt lonely without his little sister constantly chattering away to him. When he visited, we played and talked together for hours but it was not the same as being together all the time.

Every Friday night was bath night for me. Aunt Annie would heat water on the kitchen range and then I would be bathed in a zinc bath if front of the fire. I would then be dried in one of aunt Annie's lovely soft towels and she would cuddle me and laughingly say 'time for nails'- because she knew that I hated having my nails cut. However, I had to endure it and used to walk round with my fingers sticking out when it was done. Aunt Annie would say – 'Daft little thing making all that fuss.' I had such a happy time there with them all and loved them dearly for making me so welcome. But I was of course overjoyed when I was old enough to return home.

*

This chapter has been the most difficult of all for me to write because, with the exception of my brother Don, I have never spoken or written a word to anyone of our mother's illness to this day. I hope I have been able to convey our deep love for her and that how knowing her enriched our lives and made us stronger. We had to grow up quickly and had to face life without a mother's advice but she was our mum and we were proud of her.

Mum (fourth from left) with Elsie on the Sunday School Treat – before she was ill

My mother's illness was tragic and there is no doubt it had a profound effect on the whole family. The story of my childhood that I have recounted here could have been a much darker tale, had I not been part of such a wonderful community. My extended family – my aunts, uncles and indeed the whole village, rallied round to ensure that I was not troubled or distressed in any way. I also had the support of the love of my sister and brothers and my wonderful dad, who was 'my rock'- who steered me through those early years. He forgave my childish indiscretions and never failed to comfort and support me in later years. I feel very fortunate indeed to have been part of this happy family and to have had such a wonderful dad.

A pensive looking Una in 1930

This then is My Story

With the ability to send flowers by lorry to the London Market at Covent Garden and the building of the new Sugar Beet Factory at Bury St Edmunds, the fortunes of the people in West Row changed dramatically. Villagers became much more affluent and quickly recovered from the harsh years of the early thirties. As more work became available, more and more people came to the village, seeking employment. This in turn changed the village life, and it was never to return to the old ways.

In our home, there was a great deal more money coming in, which made life much easier for the whole family. My sister and brothers were all working and Don and Leslie were doing part time work, even before they left school. I was always told by my sister, Elsie, that I was very lucky because I had such an easy time - I suppose she was right in a way because I was definitely spoiled by my brothers. However, dad always made sure that I was not affected by this too much. He gave me lots of jobs to do because he believed that it was not good to lead an idle life and that much satisfaction came from doing a job well, whatever it might be.

West Row came into real prominence with the discovery of a magnificent hoard of Roman silver in a field at the end of the village by Mr. Gordon Butcher (as he was deep ploughing the field). The national press soon got hold of the story, calling it the 'Mildenhall Treasure' – which really should have been the 'West Row Treasure,' - it is now safely ensconced in the British Museum in London. There are several books telling the story of how it was found and its description.

This then is my story of how life was between the two world wars. Many, many events and people I realise are left out but, I have done my very best to convey the essence of life in a fenland village, a village that was so shortly to be catapulted into another world war and thus it would be irrevocably changed. The life we lived in the thirties has gone but, looking back over those early years, I realise they were a wonderful springboard to the joys, trials and tribulations to come. Those formative years gave us the strength to cope with whatever we were confronted with. Life was difficult and my family suffered tragic loss during those early days but we were taught 'never to despair.'

West Row was a wonderful place to be brought up in.

Appendix 1

Suffolk Harvest Cake:

        1lb White Flour

        4 ozs Corn flour

        2 Teaspoons Baking Powder

        ½ Teaspoon Bicarbonate of Soda

        Pinch Ground Nutmeg

        Pinch Ground Cinnamon

        1 oz Finely Crumbled Yeast

        1 lb Sugar

        8 ozs Lard

        ½ Pint Milk

        2 Eggs

        1 lb Currants

        4 ozs Chopped Candied Lemon Peel

Method:

Sift together flour, corn flour, baking powder, bicarbonate of Soda, Nutmeg and cinnamon. Rub in the crumbled yeast and stir in the sugar. Cut the lard into flakes and work into the dry ingredients. Beat together eggs and milk and stir them into the other ingredients. Finally stir in the currants and candied peel until the ingredients are well blended.

Put into 2 greased and lined 10 inch round tins and leave in a warm place to rise, for 30 minutes.

Cook in a cool/moderate oven.

Appendix 2

Christmas Pudding

> **5 ozs Flour**
>
> **5 ozs Breadcrumbs**
>
> **5 ozs Soft Brown Sugar**
>
> **½ lb Suet**
>
> **½ lb Raisins**
>
> **½ lb Currants**
>
> **½ lb Sultanas**
>
> **¼ lb Mixed Peel**
>
> **1 oz Ground Almonds**
>
> **2 Eggs**
>
> **½ Teaspoon Salt**
>
> **½ Teaspoon Nutmeg – or Mixed Spice**
>
> **½ Pint Old Ale (Stout)**

Method:
Mix all the ingredients together well, in a large mixing bowl.

Put the mixture into a two pint basin and cover the top with greaseproof paper.
Cut a square piece of linen from an old bed-sheet and place this over the greaseproof paper.

Tie with string around the basin (just under the rim) and then take opposite corners and tie together, using a reef knot. Repeat the process with the other two corners. (This makes it easy to pick up the pudding with kitchen tongs – especially useful when taking out of the steamer after cooking).
Put an apple into the saucepan with cold water (to prevent the build up of lime scale and to give the steam a beautiful apple aroma).
Steam the pudding for eight hours – make sure you check the water level in the saucepan regularly, to prevent it boiling dry.
Store for at least one month and steam again for a minimum of two hours before serving.

NB. this recipe makes one large Christmas Pudding